VOLUME II

Dining In-Minneapolis/St. Paul

COOKBOOK

VOLUME II

Dining In-Minneapolis/St. Paul

C O O K B O O K

A Collection of Gourmet Recipes for Complete Meals from the Minneapolis-St. Paul Area's Finest Restaurants

CARLA
WALDEMAR

Foreword by
MITCH MILLER

Peanut Butter Publishing
Mercer Island, Washington

Cover photograph by Jean Francois Stien
Cover design and illustrations by Neil Sweeney

ISBN 0-89716-120-3

CONTENTS

FOREWORD

I've always said a symphony conductor needs three things in order to be happy. One is a fine orchestra. Another is a fine hall. And the third is a fine restaurant. I've found all three in abundance on my visits to Minneapolis/St. Paul. When I say "abundance," I mean it. I've been conducting in the Twin Cities now for upwards of seventeen years. That's a lot of conducting and, necessarily, a lot of eating . . . all kinds of good music, all kinds of good food.

I like variety in food just as I like variety in music. My concerts have always featured contrasts in repertory, and so have my own personal tastes in restaurants. The Twin Cities are so rich in ethnic backgrounds and at the same time so cosmopolitan, and their food traditions are so rich as a result, that you can be as experimental in your eating experiences as you wish.

I grew up in upstate New York, my parents hard-working Jewish immigrants. Our family meals were satisfying peasant fare. Years later it was hard for me to believe that I could find that same kind of food in a young, blond state like Minnesota, but it proved to be true. And there was plenty of the equally satisfying German cooking which is akin to it. Not to mention those mouth-watering Scandinavian fish preparations; brilliant triumphs from the French cuisine; Chinese specialties as good as any I ever tasted. *And* the grass-roots kind of Midwestern American cookery which seemed to me just as exotic and appealing as those others.

Of course, I have my favorite gustatorial oases in the Twin Cities. Tor and Kristine Aasheim are old friends, and a visit to Minneapolis would be unthinkable without several meals at their delectable restaurant, La Tortue. For steaks you can't beat Murray's. I love the coffee and the butter squares at the New French Cafe. And Leeann Chin cooks up a Chinese storm. I suppose I'm a creature of habit, basically— I always intend to try a lot of new places but I generally return to the familiar spots I've learned to enjoy. I don't like to eat heartily before a concert—no musician does—so my post-concert choices are limited to those restaurants which stay open fairly late, like Rudolph's.

Twin Cities audiences love good music, and as far as I'm concerned, that automatically means they love other pleasures of the heart, mind and body, like food. No wonder good restaurants proliferate there, along with concert subscriptions. *Dining In–Minneapolis/St. Paul, Volume II* tells you about some of my favorites.

Mitch Miller

PREFACE

A decade or so ago, the Twin Cities may have rivaled London as a place to visit for its music, museums, theater, and pretty green parks and pathways—but not to dine. To eat, yes: on safe and substantial steak and potatoes, the robust fare that left our palates pleasantly satiated although unstimulated. We loved our T-bone done to a T, with the Minnesota iceberg and Idaho trimmings that signified for us Midwesterners a night on the town.

The town and the times have changed. Twin Citians began to travel more, and their taste buds were piqued by what they ate, be it the elegance of aristocratic cuisines or the eclectic delights of ethnic specialties. Travelers, too, came with increasing frequency to our towns, including a colony of young French chefs who set about revitalizing Minnesota menus and preparation standards. Hotels took note and showered us with showcase dining rooms that could rival any in the nation as pavilions of fine cuisine. The favorite long-established dining institutions paid note to patrons' increased awareness of quality in wine and viands and in their practiced service. Fledgling restaurateurs heard the message and eagerly rose to the challenge, rewarding the discerning diner with innovative menus that delivered what they promised: impeccably prepared plates in tasteful eating quarters.

I sense this excitement not only as a frequent patron and reviewer of the cities' establishments, but in speaking behind the scenes with the restaurateurs and their chefs. Their talent and imagination are equaled only by their high standards and pride in their work. Fresh fish is now a daily given, even in the landlocked heart of the Corn Belt. Vegetables are done al dente. Iceberg is matched with more adventurous greenery, bathed in herbs and oils that come from the kitchen's recipe, not the wholesaler's. And those kitchens have further come of age: they yield superior sauces, pastry that's the pride of the bread basket and dessert cart, or authentic international fare that's light-years removed from the days of take-home pizza and chow mein.

Twin Citians have turned from eating to dining even in their homes. They are investigating the mysteries of food, honing their expertise with cooking classes and doing their marketing with discernment. Now, thanks to the cooperation of the chefs and restaurateurs of the establishments included in this book, both novices and experienced cooks can duplicate in their own homes an evening of dining on the town. The menus and recipes, along with each chef's counsel and tips gleaned from years of training backed up by the school of experience, will open new dining vistas on the home front. So start stirring, phone a few friends, and bon appétit!

Carla Waldemar

THE BLUE HORSE

Dinner for Four

Beef and Tomato Consommé

Caesar Salad

Poached Paupiettes of Flounder with Champagne Sauce

Fresh d'Anjou Pears Flambé

Wines:

With the Consommé and Flounder—Far Niente Chardonnay, 1980

*With the Pears—Chateau Saint Jean Johannisberg Riesling,
Belle Terre, Late Harvest, 1977*

Clifford Warling, Owner
John Warling, General Manager
Dick Lensing, Chef

THE BLUE HORSE

We don't need to see the menu; just set something up for us," say the regular patrons of the Blue Horse, and John Warling, manager and maitre d', knows why. "Consistency in service and food have given us the ability to win their confidence. Our steady customers come in for lunch five times a week. We see the same familiar faces—that's what makes it fun!"

Some of those familiar faces have been Blue Horse devotees ever since John's father Clifford Warling left a flourishing restaurant career in Seattle to return to his hometown and open the city's first Continental-style café. Clifford introduced the Twin Cities to his West Coast favorites—Puget Sound salmon, Dungeness crab, Olympia oysters—and unveiled then-exotic specialties such as steak Diane, fettuccini Alfredo, steak tartare, Caesar salad, and flaming desserts done with tableside cart service that remain the restaurant's signature. Following his father's pioneering of fresh seafood in Minnesota, John works to keep the Blue Horse the place to go for fish. "We bring it out on a silver platter to display before cooking—ivory salmon, halibut out of Alaska, Florida grouper, gray sole from Boston. It's unbelievable! It's taking off like we never dreamed."

Dick Lensing, for years a hotel chef, brought his creative expertise to the Blue Horse two years ago. "He's doing an exceptional job," vouches John. "He's young, as I am, so we are of like minds. All of us here take an active part in planning the menu—and we listen to the customers' wishes. They call in and say, 'I'm bringing in four people tonight. Do something special!' On a busy night it kills us, but that's the fun—that personalized service. And many of our new menu items originated with those specially created dishes."

Tradition is honored in this award-winning restaurant. The supper club's decor includes arched brick walls, wood paneling hung with artwork in ornate gilt frames, and, of course, the larger-than-life stylized copper wall sculpture of a galloping steed from which the Blue Horse draws its name.

1355 University Avenue
St. Paul

BEEF AND TOMATO CONSOMMÉ

2 quarts BEEF STOCK, cold
(see next page)
8 egg whites
2 pounds coarsely ground
beef
1 (6-ounce) can tomato paste
5 to 6 juniper berries
½ teaspoon fennel seeds
1 bay leaf

½ medium-size onion, finely
chopped
3 stalks celery, finely
chopped
1 teaspoon black peppercorns
1 clove garlic, finely chopped
Salt and pepper
Fresh fennel sprigs

1. Pour the cold Beef Stock into a heavy stockpot or saucepan. In a mixing bowl, thoroughly combine the egg whites, ground beef, tomato paste, juniper berries, fennel seeds, bay leaf, onion, celery, peppercorns, and garlic. Add to the stock and mix well.
2. Bring to a boil over high heat, stirring occasionally. Immediately reduce heat and simmer gently about 3 hours, or until the stock is reduced by half. Taste for desired strength. The longer the stock simmers, the stronger it will taste. Do not break the "raft" or scum that accumulates on the surface.
3. To clarify for consommé, strain the stock into a clean pot through a sieve lined with dampened cheesecloth.
4. Reheat the consommé and season with salt and pepper. Ladle into four bowls. Garnish with the fennel sprigs and serve at once.

Here at the Blue Horse, every new sauce or wine is explained to the staff, and every new item that comes on the menu we sit down and try.

THE BLUE HORSE

BEEF STOCK

5 pounds beef shank bones, split to expose marrow

1 large onion, coarsely chopped

4 stalks celery, coarsely chopped

1 medium-size carrot, coarsely chopped

1 bay leaf

½ teaspoon peppercorns

½ teaspoon salt

½ teaspoon chopped garlic

In a large saucepan or stockpot, bring all ingredients and 2 gallons cold water to boil. Reduce heat to a low simmer. Cover and simmer gently 6 to 8 hours until reduced by half. Skim frequently to remove the scum that gathers on the surface. Strain through a sieve lined with dampened cheesecloth. Refrigerate until ready to use, or freeze, if desired.

THE BLUE HORSE

CAESAR SALAD

1 head romaine lettuce
1 clove garlic, crushed
½ teaspoon freshly ground pepper
Juice of ½ lemon
1 teaspoon Worcestershire sauce
6 anchovy fillets, chopped
1 teaspoon Dijon mustard

6 tablespoons imported olive oil
2 tablespoons French red wine vinegar
2 eggs, at room temperature
2 tablespoons butter
½ cup croutons
1 cup freshly grated Parmesan cheese (approximately)

1. Wash the romaine and pat dry. Trim and cut the length of the leaves twice, then the width at 1½-inch intervals, or tear into pieces of similar size. Set aside.

2. Rub the garlic around the bottom of a large wooden bowl; reserve the pulp. Add the pepper, lemon juice, Worcestershire sauce, and anchovies. With a fork, mash the anchovies into a fine paste against the bottom of the bowl. Add the mustard, olive oil, and vinegar; blend thoroughly.

3. To coddle the eggs, bring water in a saucepan to a boil. Gently lower the eggs in the saucepan, cover, and turn off heat. Let cook 1 minute, remove, and cool slightly. Break the eggs into a dish and beat lightly. Add to the anchovy mixture, beating vigorously until the dressing begins to thicken.

4. In a shallow frying pan, melt the butter and sauté the reserved garlic pulp. As it begins to aromatize, add the croutons and sauté until lightly browned.

5. Place the romaine in the salad bowl and toss thoroughly. Add ½ cup of the Parmesan cheese and the croutons. Toss lightly and serve on well-chilled plates. Top each portion with additional Parmesan cheese, if desired.

To prepare a tableside salad was very unusual eighteen years ago. Today Caesar Salad is still one of our more popular items, still prepared from scratch and tossed right at the table.

POACHED PAUPIETTES OF FLOUNDER
WITH CHAMPAGNE SAUCE

4 (6 to 7-ounce) flounder
   fillets
2 carrots, peeled and
   julienned
1 teaspoon sugar
¼ cup club soda
   (approximately)
16 spears asparagus
1 large cucumber
1 quart COURT BOUILLON
   (see second page following)
¼ pound butter, at
   room temperature
   (approximately)

1 teaspoon diced onion
2 tablespoons white wine
   Juice of 1 lemon
4 teaspoons chopped
   shallots
½ cup champagne
½ cup whipping cream
   Salt and pepper
1 teaspoon chopped fresh
   chervil

1. Remove cartilage from the fillets. Cut each fillet in half lengthwise. To form the paupiettes, roll the fillet halves skin side up, starting at the wide end, and secure with toothpicks. Set aside.

2. In a saucepan, place the carrots, sugar, and club soda to cover. Simmer about 2 minutes, or until barely tender. Remove carrots from pan and cover with a damp towel.

3. Lightly peel the asparagus spears and tie together in a bundle. Immerse the stems in a pan of simmering water. Cook 3 to 4 minutes, or until al dente. Remove from pan and cover with a damp towel.

4. Peel the cucumber, cut in half lengthwise, remove the seeds and slice thinly. Set aside.

5. Bring the Court Bouillon to a gentle simmer. Add the paupiettes and poach about 8 to 10 minutes, or until flaky. Check after 7 minutes. Be sure water does not boil. Remove the paupiettes from the bouillon and take out the toothpicks. Cover and keep warm in a low oven. Reserve the bouillon.

6. In a sauté pan, melt 1 tablespoon of the butter. Add the cucumber and onion and sauté over high heat about 4 to 5 minutes, stirring occasionally, or until the cucumber is al dente. Add the wine and simmer 1 minute to let the alcohol evaporate.

7. Meanwhile, melt 1 tablespoon of the butter in a steel frying pan. Sauté the asparagus spears in the butter for 2 minutes, sprinkling the lemon juice on top. In a separate pan, melt 1 tablespoon of the butter and sauté 2 teaspoons of the shallots and the carrots for 1 minute. Keep the asparagus and carrots warm.

8. In a saucepan with a heavy bottom, sauté the remaining 2 teaspoons shallots in 1 teaspoon of the butter about 1 minute. Add the champagne and ¾ cup of the reserved Court Bouillon. Cook over high heat about 4 to 5 minutes until reduced by half. Add the cream and cook 1 minute, or until the sauce has reached a light consistency. Be sure that the sauce does not come to a boil. Remove from heat, add 4 tablespoons of the butter and whisk until thoroughly blended with the sauce. Season with the salt and pepper to taste.

9. Arrange the sautéed cucumber in the center of four dinner plates. Place two paupiettes on the cucumber portions. Pour the champagne sauce equally over the paupiettes and sprinkle with the chopped chervil. For garnish, arrange the asparagus spears and the carrots next to the paupiettes on each plate. Drizzle the warm lemon-flavored butter over the spears. Serve at once before the champagne sauce has a chance to curdle.

Note: Sole may be substituted freely for the flounder.

We never expected the success we've had with fresh fish. The reason for it? We find people have become very diet-conscious—and they enjoy the concept of 'fresh.'

THE BLUE HORSE

COURT BOUILLON

½ cup white wine
½ cup white vinegar
¼ cup diced onion
⅛ cup diced celery

2 tablespoons diced carrot
1 bay leaf
⅛ teaspoon salt
6 peppercorns

Place all ingredients with 3 cups cold water in a saucepan. Simmer ½ hour to blend flavors; do not reduce. Refrigerate or freeze, as desired.

FRESH D'ANJOU PEARS FLAMBÉ

2 fresh d'Anjou pears
1 tablespoon butter
⅓ cup sugar
   Juice of 1 lime
1 cup melba sauce
   (purchased)

¼ cup port wine
2 tablespoons brandy
1 pint French vanilla
   ice cream
½ cup sliced almonds

1. Cut each pear into six equal portions and peel. Plunge the pears into boiling water and cook about 4 to 10 minutes, or until they begin to soften but are still firm. Do not overcook. Remove the pears and cover with a damp cloth to prevent discoloration. Set aside.

2. In a shallow frying pan placed over high heat, melt the butter and sugar together. Add the lime juice and the melba sauce. Blend together with a fork until the sauce becomes smooth. Return to a boil for 2 to 3 minutes.

3. Add the port to the melba sauce mixture and blend well; add the pears. In a butter warmer or other long-handled saucepan, warm the brandy over low heat; ignite with a match. Drizzle over the pears in the pan. Continue to cook the pears over high heat until they are fork tender.

4. While the pears are cooking, place one scoop of the ice cream on each of four dessert plates. Remove the cooked pears from the sauce and place over the scoops of ice cream.

5. Reduce the sauce over high heat about 2 minutes, or until it begins to thicken. Immediately spoon over the pears and ice cream. Top with the sliced almonds and serve at once.

This dessert is as much fun to prepare as it is to eat. It's simple, but it never fails to impress.

Dinner for Six

Ballottine de Caneton

Filet de Sole Bonne Femme

Cailles Rôties aux Raisins

Filet à la Moutarde

Garniture de Légumes

Salade d'Endive de Belgique

Mousse aux Fraises

Wines:
With the Ballottine—Fleurie, Beaujolais, 1978
With the Sole—Clos Ste. Magdeleine, 1978
With the Cailles Rôties—Château Bon Dieu des Vignes, 1977
With the Filet—Château Vignelaure, 1977
With the Mousse—Coteaux du Layon, 1978

John Lehodey, General Manager
Cynthia Johnson, Director of Catering
Daniel Hubert, Executive Chef

LE CAFE ROYAL

lassic haute cuisine in a decidedly Parisienne setting: c'est Le Cafe Royal, the formal dining room of L'hotel Sofitel. Leave the trendy to someone else; it is tradition that is honored here. The fin de siecle decor bespeaks elegance. Moss green carpeting matches the greenery of potted palms. Dainty handwrought provincial furniture is set against tables draped with white. Softly burnished golden walls return the sparkle of the mirrored ceiling. And the service is as polished as the setting—utterly elegant, utterly French.

So also is the chef. Young Daniel Hubert first trained with his father, a restaurateur in northern France, before serving his formal apprenticeship which led him to kitchens in Geneva, Paris, and finally the Sofitel, where he has been head chef since its opening in 1975. Chef Daniel rules his kitchen in the style in which he was schooled, the classic regime of Escoffier. "It's like the Bible: we don't ask why it's done like this, but we all do it. There are really no secrets in cooking. Even nouvelle cuisine is not new. Someone has always done it before—it's the touch of the person who prepares it that makes the difference."

Vive la différence at Le Cafe. Half of the menu features classic French dishes such as sole bonne femme, sweetbreads with a Medici garnish, and coquille St. Jacques. The remaining courses are changed weekly to honor a special region of France and to take advantage of the seasonal seafood flown in from the Continent like langoustines, scallops, and escargots. "Even the Dover sole comes from the French side of the channel," Daniel proudly states. To complement this exquisite cuisine, General Manager John Lehodey frequently tours his French homeland to purchase boutique wines, many of which are specially bottled for the hotel. John explains, "We try to authentically represent every region in France; we pride ourselves on those wines."

Undoubtedly, they also pride themselves on the skill of the staff. There is more than a touch of showmanship in the tableside presentations, from slicing of pâtés off a pheasant-dressed display to skillful boning of a trout, from preparation of a dazzling flambé to careful piloting of a dessert trolley. The etiquette affirms that, at Le Cafe, diners experience a world apart.

L'hotel Sofitel
4501 West 78th Street
Bloomington

LE CAFE ROYAL

BALLOTTINE DE CANETON

1 (4-pound) duck	2 tablespoons minced onion
1 pound lard	2 teaspoons minced parsley
¼ cup cognac	2 cloves garlic, minced
½ teaspoon grated nutmeg	¼ cup port or Madeira
Salt and pepper	2 small eggs
1 packet Knox gelatin	2 tablespoons pistachios
1 cup canned beef consommé	or truffles
6 ounces veal	6 large leaves Boston lettuce
6 ounces pork	12 cornichons
2 tablespoons minced shallots	

1. A day or two in advance, debone the duck by placing it breast side down on a cutting board and making a deep incision the length of the duck on one side of the backbone. Loosen the meat from the carcass by scraping close to the bone with the point of a sharp paring knife. Carefully pull meat away from the bone, cutting through the cartilage between back and breastbone. Debone one side of the duck to the breastbone, then repeat the process on the other side, taking care not to tear the skin. Remove the backbone and the bones from the breast. To remove the leg and wing bones, cut around the joints and scrape the meat down the bones. Carefully remove the skin and refrigerate for later use. Set aside the meat. Discard the bones, carcass, and giblets.

2. Cut the duck meat and one-fourth of the lard into thick strips. Place in a bowl and pour 2 tablespoons of the cognac over. Sprinkle with ¼ teaspoon of the nutmeg and season with a pinch each of salt and pepper. Let marinate overnight in refrigerator.

3. The next day, make aspic by sprinkling the gelatin over the surface of ½ cup of the consommé; let soak 3 minutes without stirring. Bring the remaining ½ cup consommé to a boil and add to the soaked gelatin. Stir until dissolved; let cool.

4. In a meat grinder or food processor, grind the remaining lard together with the veal and pork. In a small bowl, combine the ground mixture with the shallots, onion, parsley, and garlic. Add the remaining 2 tablespoons cognac and the port or Madeira; stir well. Add the eggs and the pistachios or truffles. Season with salt, pepper, and the remaining ¼ teaspoon nutmeg. Combine thoroughly.

(continued next page)

5. Preheat oven to 400°.

6. Trim the fat from the reserved duck skin. Line the bottom and sides of a terrine with three-fourths of the skin. Spread the marinated duck/lard mixture and the veal/pork/lard forcemeat in alternating layers to fill the terrine. Cover with the remaining duck skin so the filling is protected while baking.

7. Set the terrine inside a larger pan filled halfway with warm water. Bake in preheated oven for 1½ hours.

8. When done, remove the terrine and pour off the grease; let cool. Pour the half-set aspic jelly into the terrine and set a plate on top to weight down. Refrigerate 8 hours or overnight.

9. Place the lettuce leaves on six chilled plates. Cut the cold ballottine in ½-inch thick slices and arrange attractively on the leaves. Garnish with the cornichons and serve.

Note: If chopped jelled aspic is desired for garnish, make additional aspic according to directions in step 3 and chill until set.

Cornichons are imported French gherkins.

Was Minneapolis ready for French food? At first we sold two dozen escargot a week. Today we sell fifty! And the baguettes? We bake twelve hundred each day. They are a natural accompaniment for the ballottine.

FILET DE SOLE BONNE FEMME

3 large fresh sole
5 tablespoons butter
  (approximately)
3 tablespoons chopped onion
3 tablespoons chopped carrot
½ cup chopped shallots
  Bouquet garni:
    1 parsley sprig
    1 sprig celery leaves
    1 bay leaf
    1 leek stem

3 tablespoons flour
  Salt and pepper
½ pound fresh mushrooms,
  washed and sliced
2 tablespoons chopped
  parsley
1 scant cup dry white wine
2 cups whipping cream
  Juice of 1 lemon

1. Remove the skin from each sole. With a sharp knife, make four fillets of each by cutting in half lengthwise near the center bone, then again cutting each half in two strips. Remove the bones with the tip of the knife. Pound the fillets lightly to flatten and break the nerves. Rinse in cold water. Clean and chop the bones, rinse in cold water, and set aside.

2. To make a fish stock, heat 1 tablespoon of the butter in a saucepan. Add the onion, carrot, ¼ cup of the shallots, and the chopped fish bones and cook until the vegetables begin to release their juices. Cover with water, add the bouquet garni, and cook over medium heat for 20 minutes, skimming often. Strain the stock through a sieve lined with dampened cheesecloth and return to pan.

3. Make a roux by mixing 3 tablespoons of the butter with the flour in a small bowl. Add the roux to the fish stock, stirring constantly. Cook this sauce over medium high heat for 25 minutes.

4. Preheat oven to 400°.

5. While the fish sauce is cooking, place the fillets bone side down and fold over once. Butter a 9-inch by 12-inch baking pan, and sprinkle it with ½ teaspoon salt and ¼ teaspoon pepper. Place the folded fillets in the baking pan. Arrange the remaining ¼ cup shallots and the mushrooms around the fillets. Sprinkle with the parsley and season with salt and pepper, if desired. Pour the wine over the fillets. Place the pan over high heat and bring to a boil. Remove and bake in preheated oven 5 to 10 minutes, or until the fillets flake easily. Remove from oven.

6. Butter a serving platter. Place the fillets and mushrooms on the platter; cover with waxed paper to keep warm. Pour the bouillon from the baking pan into a small saucepan and cook over medium heat until reduced by half. Stir in the cream and lemon juice and season with salt and pepper. Add the simmering fish sauce to the bouillon and stir to blend. Strain through a fine sieve. Pour over the fillets and serve at once.

Ten years ago you couldn't find ten pounds of fresh ocean fish in Minnesota. Today we sell more fish than meat! Fish is more creative to cook with—there are many more recipes for fish than for lamb and beef.

LE CAFE ROYAL

CAILLES RÔTIES AUX RAISINS

1 cup dried raisins	4 teaspoons pepper
¼ cup brandy	½ pound butter, at room
12 quails	temperature
¼ cup salt	¾ cup dry white wine

1. Place the raisins and brandy in a bowl and add enough water to cover. Soak for 1 hour.
2. Preheat oven to 450°.
3. Clean the quails and truss wings and legs to body with string. Season the inside and outside generously with the salt and pepper. Spread about 1 tablespoon of the butter evenly over each. Arrange in a roasting pan and roast in preheated oven 25 to 30 minutes.
4. Remove the baking pan from the oven. Remove the quails and keep warm on a serving platter. Deglaze the pan over medium heat by adding the wine and ¾ cup water, then stirring and scraping the solidified pan juices. Cook approximately 10 minutes, or until reduced by half. Add the remaining 4 tablespoons butter and stir until well blended. Strain the sauce through a sieve into a bowl.
5. Drain the raisins, discarding liquid. Stir the raisins into the sauce. Place two quails each on six dinner plates. Pour the raisin sauce over and serve at once.

The simple things are the best. There is no need to spend hours cooking every dish.

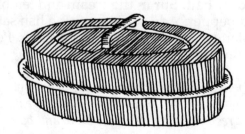

FILET A LA MOUTARDE

4 tablespoons butter, at
  room temperature
6 (8-ounce) filets mignons
2 shallots
1 cup dry white wine
½ cup whipping cream
3 tablespoons Dijon
  mustard

Fines herbes:
1 sprig parsley, finely
  chopped
1 sprig chervil, finely
  chopped
1 green onion stem, finely
  chopped
1 sprig thyme, finely
  chopped

1. Heat the butter in a sauté pan until it sizzles. Sauté the filets over high heat until juice begins to appear on the surface, then turn and brown on other side. Remove from pan, place on a serving platter, and keep warm.

2. Sauté the shallots in the butter remaining in the pan about 1 minute; do not brown. Add the wine and reduce about ½ minute to let alcohol evaporate. Add the cream and cook over medium heat approximately 5 minutes until reduced by half. Add the mustard and the fines herbes. Stir well. Pour the sauce over the filets and serve at once with the Garniture de Légumes.

Nouvelle cuisine? It depends on the quantity you eat, not the ingredients, to be healthy and feel good. I prefer the classic sauces and garnitures of Escoffier.

GARNITURE DE LÉGUMES

2 *dozen small, young turnips, peeled*	2 *dozen pearl onions, peeled*
2 *dozen baby carrots, peeled*	4 *tablespoons butter*

1. Carve the turnips and carrots into seven-sided oval shapes each 2 inches long. In a saucepan, bring to boil just enough salted water to cover the vegetables. Add the turnips, carrots, and onions. Cook 6 to 8 minutes, or until al dente. Immediately remove from high heat and strain well.
2. In a frying pan, melt the butter and sauté the vegetables 2 to 3 minutes over medium heat; do not let brown. Remove and serve at once.

SALADE D'ENDIVE DE BELGIQUE

2 *tablespoons vinegar*	¾ *cup salad oil*
Salt	6 *Belgian endives*
Freshly ground black pepper	

1. Pour the vinegar into a jar with a screw-top lid, and season with salt and pepper to taste. Add the oil and set aside.
2. Peel the endives and wipe each leaf with a clean, damp linen towel. Arrange the leaves over six salad plates.
3. Before serving, secure the lid to the jar of vinegar dressing. Shake well and drizzle over the endives. Serve at once.

When making the oil and vinegar dressing, always remember to use one volume of vinegar to five times as much oil, and add the salt and pepper to the vinegar, never to the oil or to the oil and vinegar mixture.

Our endive is flown in fresh. Make sure when selecting yours that the leaves are young and delicate.

LE CAFE ROYAL

MOUSSE AUX FRAISES

1 quart strawberries, washed and hulled (approximately)	⅔ cup sugar
1 tablespoon gelatin	1¼ cups whipping cream
2 eggs, separated	¼ cup strawberry liqueur

1. Reserve 6 strawberries for garnish. Press the rest through a sieve to obtain 1¼ cups pulp. Set aside. Soften the gelatin in ½ cup cold water. Pour into a small pan and warm over low heat to dissolve. Set aside.
2. In a small bowl, beat the egg yolks and one-third of the sugar with electric beaters until smooth. Combine the strawberry pulp and the dissolved gelatin with the beaten yolks. Set aside.
3. In a separate bowl, beat the egg whites with electric beaters until soft peaks form. Gradually add the remaining sugar, a few tablespoons at a time, continuing to beat until stiff peaks form.
4. In a well-chilled bowl, whip the cream until firm. Set aside. Add the liqueur to the strawberry mixture. With a spatula, fold the whipped cream into this mixture just until blended. Then lightly fold in the egg whites. Pour the mousse into six dessert dishes and chill at least 1 hour. Before serving, garnish each dish with a fresh strawberry.

Here we adhere to the classic preparation methods and presentation style, just as I was trained to do so in France.

SINCE 1978

Dinner for Six

Foie Gras Mousse

Mushroom Consommé

Baked Red Snapper in Romaine

Warm Scallop and Cucumber Salad

Grand Marnier Soufflé

Wines:

*With the Mousse and Consommé—Robert Pecota
Sauvignon Blanc, 1980*

With the Snapper—Burgess Cellars Chardonnay, 1978

With the Salad—Cold Springs sparkling water

With the Soufflé—Tokaji Azsu Five Puttonos

*Gordon Schutte, Owner
Sidney Larson, Executive Chef*

THE 510 HAUTE CUISINE

I 've forever been a devotee of food and wines," confesses Gordon Schutte, owner of the 510 Haute Cuisine. He has not, however, always been a restaurateur. He was a successful businessman until October of 1978, when his restaurant opened on the ground floor of 510 Groveland, a patrician residential hotel. "I thought the time was right; there were then very few restaurants of high caliber here in Minneapolis. My own preference is for French cuisine, so that's the direction we decided to go—to offer a unique cuisine and style of service in an atmosphere that, too, is unique."

The charming rococo decor of the restaurant is also unusual. Dainty moldings, gracefully draped windows, and beaded chandeliers have been retained from the days of the room's former grandeur, today updated by subtle tones of pearl gray and deeper charcoal, by mirror tiles, and by tasteful touches of growing greens. In this resplendent setting, the serving staff, attired in evening dress, present themselves with a successful blend of friendliness and formality. "We want to see that our guests are served very good food very well," pronounces the 510's genial host. "We ask them to do a great deal more for us than many places would. They see the owner getting his own hands dirty, so they gain an immediate sense of what's happening around the restaurant and want to do it even better."

That mix of loyalty and freedom is epitomized in the 510's young chef, Sidney Larsen, whose trademarks are curiosity, creativity, and taste. "You can't teach those," avers his mentor. "Those are the real marks of a chef. For them I would trade all the great training from the Continent. Sidney's quite experimental. He tends to have a light hand at seasonings and sauces. He's just tremendous at the art of delicate stock making, and that's the heart of a kitchen. He's got half a dozen kinds, some of the richest flavorings I've ever tasted, and they appear all over the menu in soups, meats, sauces. . . ."

This ode to consummate cuisine is borne out in the tasting. The 510's menu boasts such a meal as mushroom mousse that delights even hardened connoisseurs, pâtés and terrines as lovely in their presentation as in their taste, a palate-cleansing homemade sorbet to follow, and then perhaps lamb en croûte Florentine or sliced duck breast with green peppercorns. "We don't put anything on the table that we haven't done ourselves. There's total integrity in what we do."

510 Groveland Avenue
Minneapolis

FOIE GRAS MOUSSE

1 (4-ounce) can foie gras
1 small shallot, minced
¼ pound chicken breast,
  skinned, boned, and
  coarsely diced
¼ cup cognac
2 tablespoons Madeira
1 cup whipping cream

¼ teaspoon salt
  Pinch of white pepper
½ loaf French bread
  (preferably day-old)
4 tablespoons butter
  PÉRIGUEUX SAUCE
  (see next page)

1. Drain the fat from the can of fois gras into a small sauté pan. Over medium heat, sauté the shallot, foie gras, and chicken in this fat about 3 minutes, or until just brown. Add the cognac and Madeira and simmer over low heat about 2 minutes, or until the liquid is reduced by half.

2. In a separate small pan, reduce the cream by one-fourth. Place the foie gras mixture and the reduced cream into an electric blender and blend until the mixture is silky smooth and fluffy. Season with the salt and pepper, and blend.

3. To make croutons, cut the bread into twelve ½-inch slices. Heat the butter in a sauté pan and sauté the slices on both sides until golden.

4. Spread the mousse on the croutons and arrange on a serving plate. Serve at room temperature garnished with the Périgueux Sauce.

The mousse can be served in other ways: scooped into individual serving dishes or molded. To create a mold, turn the prepared mousse into a lightly-buttered form, chill several hours, and unmold by wrapping the form with a tea towel dipped in hot water and wrung nearly dry. However you choose to serve it, be sure the foie gras mousse is at room temperature to attain utmost flavor.

PÉRIGUEUX SAUCE

3 tablespoons truffles, minced
3 tablespoons unsalted butter
Pinch of salt

Scant pinch of white pepper
¼ cup Madeira
1 cup VEAL DEMI-GLACE

1. In a small sauté pan, gently sauté the truffles in 1 tablespoon of the butter for 1 minute. Season with the salt, white pepper, and 1 tablespoon of the Madeira. Drain the truffles, reserving the juice. Set aside.

2. In a saucepan, combine the juice reserved from the truffles with the Veal Demi-Glace. Over very low heat, bring to a gentle simmer. Simmer 6 to 8 minutes. Add the truffles. Whisk in the remaining 2 tablespoons butter and the remaining 3 tablespoons Madeira. Serve at room temperature over the Foie Gras Mousse.

VEAL DEMI-GLACE

2½ pounds veal knuckle,
   cut in chunks
1 large onion, sliced
2 carrots, sliced
1 stalk celery, sliced
1 clove garlic, chopped

Bouquet garni:
   1 sprig thyme
   1 sprig parsley
   1 sprig rosemary
   1 bay leaf
2 teaspoons tomato paste

1. Preheat oven to 475°.
2. Place the veal knuckle in a shallow roasting pan and roast in preheated oven 45 minutes, or until very brown. Remove the knuckle and set aside. Place the onion, carrots, celery, and garlic in the roasting pan. Stir to coat well with the roasting fat, then roast at 475° about 15 minutes until browned.
3. When the vegetables are browned, strain and discard the fat. Place the vegetables and knuckle in a 4-quart stockpot with the bouquet garni and tomato paste. Cover the bottom of the roasting pan with water and bring to a boil over high heat, scraping the solidified pan juices, then pour into the stockpot.
4. Add water to the stockpot to cover the knuckle and bring to a vigorous boil over high heat; reduce heat to a simmer. Skim the fat and scum off the top and simmer about 4 hours, replacing the evaporated liquid after the first two hours and skimming every 15 minutes.
5. Strain into a heavy pan through a fine sieve. Reduce to 1 cup; the stock will have a thickened, syrupy viscosity. Remove from heat and keep warm.

The Veal Demi-Glace, properly thickened, is the vital ingredient to the Périgueux Sauce. Prepared veal demi-glace may also be purchased in gourmet food shops.

MUSHROOM CONSOMMÉ

1⅛ pounds mushrooms,
    washed and wiped dry
1 tomato, finely chopped
2 shallots, finely chopped
1 clove garlic, finely chopped
2 tablespoons butter
1 cup Madeira
1 cup dry white wine
1 quart CHICKEN STOCK
    Juice of ½ lemon

3 sprigs parsley
3 peppercorns
1 sprig thyme
1 sprig rosemary
4 coriander seeds
1 small bay leaf
3 egg whites
3 egg shells, crushed
½ teaspoon salt

1. Finely chop 1 pound of the mushrooms, reserving 6 whole ones for garnish. In a sauté pan, sauté the mushrooms, tomato, shallots, and garlic in the butter until softened.

2. In a 4-quart saucepan, place the Madeira, white wine, Chicken Stock, lemon juice, parsley, peppercorns, thyme, rosemary, coriander, and bay leaf. Lightly beat the egg whites and the shells with the salt, then add to the pot. Add the sautéed ingredients and bring mixture to a quick simmer over moderately high heat, stirring constantly until the simmer is reached; then discontinue stirring. Cook for 45 minutes.

3. Strain into a clean pot through a sieve lined with dampened cheesecloth. Adjust salt to taste.

4. Pour water into a small sauté pan to a depth of ½ inch and warm. Slice the reserved whole mushrooms and poach about 1 minute. Drain.

5. Ladle the consommé into individual serving bowls and garnish with the poached mushrooms. Serve at once.

Note: Blanched, julienned leeks may be substituted for the mushroom garnish.

If there's a capsule phrase that envelops us, it's honesty in preparation. We don't use frozen, canned, or "stretcher" foods.

CHICKEN STOCK

2 pounds chicken bones	1 bay leaf
1 stalk celery, chopped	3 to 4 peppercorns
1 carrot, chopped	1 tablespoon salt
½ onion, chopped	

1. Place the chicken bones, celery, carrot, onion, bay leaf, peppercorns, and salt in a stockpot with 2½ quarts water. Bring to a boil, reduce heat and simmer 1½ hours, or until reduced to 1 quart. Skim the fat from the surface occasionally.
2. Remove the chicken bones and bay leaf. Strain the stock through a fine sieve, pushing the vegetables through for extra flavoring. Refrigerate to allow remaining fat to congeal; remove fat and discard.

BAKED RED SNAPPER IN ROMAINE

6 romaine leaves	¼ cup julienned carrot
6 (6-ounce) red snapper fillets	¼ cup julienned leek
1½ teaspoons salt	¼ cup julienned celery
½ teaspoon pepper	¼ cup julienned fennel bulb
Juice of 2 lemons	6 ounces butter
	RED BELL PEPPER SAUCE (see next page)

1. Preheat oven to 400°.
2. Steep the romaine leaves in hot water for 2 minutes. Drain and place side-by-side on tabletop. Place a snapper fillet on each leaf toward the stem end. Sprinkle the salt, pepper, and lemon juice equally over the fillets.
3. In a small saucepan, bring 1 cup water to boil; blanch the julienned carrot, leek, celery, and fennel about 1 minute, then remove and drain. Distribute the vegetables equally on the fillets and place 1 tablespoon of the butter on top of each vegetable mound.
4. Roll the romaine into bundles which enclose the fish and vegetables. Place them in an oven-proof 8-inch by 10-inch casserole. Melt the remaining butter and brush over the surface.
5. Bake, covered, in preheated oven for 15 minutes. Serve hot with Red Bell Pepper Sauce.

RED BELL PEPPER SAUCE

2 red bell peppers, cored
1 cup white wine
1 cup WHITE FISH STOCK
2 shallots, minced

2 cups whipping cream
Juice of ½ lemon
2 tablespoons unsalted butter
Salt and white pepper

1. Preheat broiler.
2. Spear the red peppers on a long cooking fork, then burn their skins under the broiler about 2 to 3 minutes, or until they blister. Remove and peel.
3. In a 1-quart saucepan, place the wine, White Fish Stock, shallots, and peeled peppers. Boil over high heat to reduce until only 2 to 3 tablespoons of liquid remain. Be careful not to scorch.
4. Add the cream and cook at a brisk simmer until the mixture is thick enough to lightly coat the back of a spoon.
5. Pour the sauce into an electric blender and purée, adding the lemon juice and butter. Add salt and pepper to taste. Return to saucepan and keep warm over very low heat until ready to serve.

WHITE FISH STOCK

2 pounds white fish bones
  and trimmings
1 stalk celery, chopped
1 carrot, chopped
½ onion, chopped

Juice of 1½ lemons
1 bay leaf
3 to 4 peppercorns
1 tablespoon salt

Place the fish bones and trimmings, celery, carrot, onion, lemon juice, bay leaf, peppercorns, and salt with 2½ quarts water into a stockpot. Bring to a boil, reduce heat and simmer 1½ hours, occasionally skimming the fat and scum that rises to the surface. Strain into a clean pot through a sieve lined with dampened cheesecloth.

WARM SCALLOP AND CUCUMBER SALAD

1 head romaine lettuce
2 cucumbers, peeled
½ cup unsalted butter
1 pound scallops
1 shallot, minced
¼ cup strawberry vinegar
½ cup dry white wine

¼ cup whipping cream
Juice of ½ lemon
Salt and pepper to taste
1 tablespoon parsley, minced
½ cup diced red bell pepper (optional)

1. Wash and shred the romaine. Split the cucumbers lengthwise and scrape out seeds with a spoon. Slice into thin slices.
2. Using one large plate, line the rim with layered cucumber slices, reserving 1 cup. Mound the shredded romaine in the center.
3. Melt the butter in a sauté pan and sauté the scallops 5 to 6 minutes. Drain, reserving butter. Place the scallops on top of the romaine on the serving plate.
4. In the empty pan, place the shallot, vinegar, wine, cream, and reserved cucumber. Boil over medium-high heat about 5 minutes, or until the liquid is reduced by one-third. Reduce heat and season with the lemon juice, salt, pepper, and parsley. Mix in the reserved butter and pour over the scallops. If desired, garnish with the diced red bell pepper. Serve at once.

We do every single plate—even for large parties—as if it's destined for a table for two. Every plate is freshly sauced or garnished just as it is served.

GRAND MARNIER SOUFFLÉ

3 tablespoons sugar
¼ pound white chocolate
¼ cup Grand Marnier
¾ cup whipping cream
   Zest of 2 oranges
5 egg yolks
2 tablespoons butter
   (approximately)

7 egg whites, at room
   temperature
   Pinch of salt
3 tablespoons confectioners'
   sugar
   ORANGE SAUCE

1. In a saucepan, place 1 tablespoon of the sugar, the chocolate, Grand Marnier, cream, and orange zest. Bring to a simmer, whisking constantly. Continuing to whisk, add the yolks one at a time. Reduce heat and simmer, stirring constantly, until the custard becomes thick enough to coat a spoon.
2. Strain the custard through a sieve into a mixing bowl and allow to cool slightly.
3. Preheat oven to 425°. Butter six one-cup soufflé dishes and sprinkle with the remaining 2 tablespoons sugar.
4. In a very clean bowl, whip the egg whites with the salt until soft peaks form. Fold the whites into the custard and gently pour or ladle the mixture into the prepared soufflé dishes.
5. Put soufflés into oven on the middle rack and reduce temperature to 365°. Bake for 10 minutes. The tops should turn golden brown.
6. Remove and dust tops with the confectioners' sugar. Serve immediately with Orange Sauce.

ORANGE SAUCE

2½ cups sugar
½ cup orange juice
½ cup Grand Marnier

¼ cup brandy
½ cup whipping cream, chilled

1. In a heavy saucepan, combine the sugar and ⅓ cup water and boil until the mixture turns a deep golden color. If necessary, wash sugar crystals off the sides of the pan with a pastry brush dipped in cold water.
2. Meanwhile, mix the orange juice, Grand Marnier, and brandy in a small pan and bring to a boil. Remove from heat.
3. When the sugar turns brown, pour in the Grand Marnier mixture and continue to cook 3 to 4 minutes longer, until the syrup is an even consistency. Cool.
4. While the syrup is cooling, whip the cream with chilled bowl and beaters until stiff. Gently fold the whipped cream into the syrup. Serve a heaping spoonful on the side of each serving of the soufflé.

Our desserts are the classics: tortes, tarts, and creams. They are probably lighter than some. Not a lot of marzipan, but pure ingredients—gorgeous stuff!

Gasthaus Bavarian Hunter

Dinner for Six

Bayrische Leberknödelsuppe

Wiener Sauerbraten

Rotkraut

Bayrischer Kartoffelsalat

Schwarzwälder Kirschtorte

Beverages:

With the Leberknödelsuppe—Bernkasteler Riesling
With the Sauerbraten—German beer
With the Kirschtorte—Jägermeister Goldwasser

Karl Schöne, Proprietor and Host
Karl Schöne, Jr. Proprietor and Chef

GASTHAUS BAVARIAN HUNTER

Crowning a pine-covered hill near the St. Croix River is the Gasthaus Bavarian Hunter—not quite an Alpine chalet, but the closest thing to it, swears its German-born proprietor, chef, and host Karl Schöne. "I didn't hire an architect or designer. Everything you see here I did myself. I wanted a German restaurant just like those in Bavaria. Customers who have been to the Black Forest tell me, 'I could have saved the plane fare!'"

The Schönes came here from Germany twenty years ago but didn't leave behind their longing for the schnitzel, sauerbraten, and sachertortes served in their family's restaurants in the homeland. They decided to duplicate that good German food in Minnesota. "People predicted I wouldn't make it, but I didn't listen." Sixteen years later those folks are eating their words and, with gusto, Karl's hearty Wagnerian fare.

The beamed chalet is furnished in the homey decor of Deutschland: imported homespun coverings for the tables, wooden booths big enough to share, carved beer kegs resting on the tiny bar, and a miscellany of stags' heads, beer steins, and Bavarian mementos lining the half-timbered walls. Strolling accordion players in Alpine hiking shorts finger the notes of "Edelweiss" while waitresses in Bavarian dirndls wind their way among the crowded tables bearing foaming mugs of German beer.

"I am very much a demanding person," says Schöne, a stickler for quality and authenticity. He personally selects the extensive list of wines, beers, and liqueurs in Germany, as well as cheeses, herring, Black Forest smoked ham, condiments, and the twenty-eight herbs that blend in the salad's vinaigrette. "Whenever I go back to Germany, I see what's tops: I like to keep up. I collect most of my recipes from the chefs of the best German restaurants. I am impressed when somebody can do something in a little different direction. I never will brag about it, but my Gasthaus is one of the best.

"A good cook must have patience," says Karl, who has imparted his kitchen skills to young Karl Jr., now co-owner of the Hunter and overseer of its kitchen. To gild the pork hocks, there are desserts lovingly crafted by Denise, Karl's wife and favorite waitress.

8390 Lofton Avenue North
Stillwater

GASTHAUS BAVARIAN HUNTER

BAYRISCHE LEBERKNÖDELSUPPE

½ pound beef or pork liver
2 strips bacon
½ cup milk
4 slices white bread
2 tablespoons butter
1 medium-size onion, chopped

1 egg
Salt and pepper
½ cup flour (approximately)
3 cups Beef Stock, hot (see index)
½ cup chopped fresh parsley

1. In a meat grinder or food processor, grind the liver and bacon and place in a large bowl.
2. In another bowl, combine the milk with ½ cup water. Add the bread slices and soak about 5 minutes. Squeeze dry, add to the ground liver and bacon, and combine well.
3. In a sauté pan, heat the butter until it sizzles. Add the onion and sauté until tender. To the liver/bacon mixture, add the sautéed onion, egg, salt and pepper to taste, and the flour as needed to bind. Combine thoroughly and let stand about 15 minutes.
4. Bring a large pan of salted water to a boil. Shape dumplings with a spoon and poach in the boiling water, a few at a time, for about 10 minutes. Drain.
5. Place the dumplings in six soup bowls. Ladle the hot beef stock into each bowl and garnish with the parsley. Serve at once.

This is standard fare in Bavaria. You don't need much beef stock. It's the liver that creates the taste. Serve the soup very hot; that's the main thing.

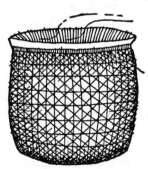

GASTHAUS BAVARIAN HUNTER

WIENER SAUERBRATEN

½ cup vinegar
½ cup dry red wine
1 medium-size onion, sliced
2 bay leaves
1 teaspoon peppercorns
1 tablespoon brown sugar
1 tablespoon soy sauce
2 pounds boneless beef roast
   (top or bottom round)
2 to 3 cloves garlic, slashed
2 teaspoons salt

Pepper
3 tablespoons shortening
½ cup chopped celery
½ cup chopped carrot
½ cup chopped onion
3 tablespoons dry bread
   crumbs
2 tablespoons flour
2 tablespoons whipping
   cream

1. Three days before serving, prepare a marinade by combining the first seven ingredients with 2 cups water. Bring to a boil, remove from heat, and cool.

2. Rub the beef with the garlic cloves, salt, and pepper to taste. Place the beef and the marinade in a medium-size bowl or one just large enough to hold the ingredients. Let stand three days.

3. After three days, remove the beef from the marinade and pat dry with a paper towel. Strain the marinade and reserve the liquid, discarding the spices and onion.

4. Preheat oven to 350°.

5. Heat the shortening in a heavy casserole and brown the beef on all sides. Remove the beef; add the celery, carrot, and onion to the casserole and cook over medium heat for 5 minutes. Add the bread crumbs. Stirring constantly, cook for 2 to 3 minutes, or until they begin to brown. Pour in 2 cups of the reserved marinade and ½ cup water. Bring to a boil. Return the beef to the casserole and cover tightly. Remove.

6. Bake in preheated oven about 2 hours, adding more of the marinade if necessary.

7. When it is done, remove the meat to a platter and keep warm in a low oven. Skim the fat off the stock in the casserole. Strain it through a sieve lined with dampened cheesecloth, then pour into a liquid measure to obtain 2½ cups. If there is too much stock, boil to reduce to correct amount; if more liquid is needed, add marinade.

8. Stir the flour into the cream to mix well. Reheat the stock in a sauce-pan. Add the flour/cream mixture, stirring constantly, until the sauce thickens.

9. Carve the beef into ¼-inch thick slices and arrange on a serving platter. Moisten with some of the sauce and serve at once. Serve the remaining sauce separately in a sauceboat.

The purpose of the marinade is not to make the beef and sauce sour but to tenderize a less expensive cut of meat. Pork and game can also be prepared in the same way.

ROTKRAUT

3 tablespoons oil or bacon drippings	2 sour apples, cored and chopped
1 small onion, chopped	1 bay leaf, crushed
1 medium-size head red cabbage, shredded	¾ teaspoon caraway seeds Salt and pepper
¼ cup vinegar	

1. In a large sauté pan with a tight-fitting lid, heat the oil. Sauté the onion for 4 minutes, or until limp. Add the cabbage and cook about 10 minutes, stirring well.

2. Add the vinegar, ½ cup water, apples, bay leaf, caraway, and salt and pepper to taste. Cover tightly and cook over low heat for 25 to 30 minutes.

3. Serve hot in a large serving dish to accompany the Wiener Sauerbraten; or, if preferred, serve as a garnish on one side of the meat platter.

I send my waitresses to Bavaria to observe not only the food but the gasthaus Gemütlichkeit.

GASTHAUS BAVARIAN HUNTER

BAYRISCHER KARTOFFELSALAT

9 medium-size boiling potatoes (approximately 3 pounds)
½ pound bacon, finely diced
½ cup chopped onion
¼ cup vinegar

½ cup Beef Stock (see index)
½ teaspoon salt
¼ teaspoon pepper
2 tablespoons finely chopped parsley

1. Boil the unpeeled potatoes about 10 minutes, or until they show only the slightest resistance when pierced with the point of a sharp knife. Drain, peel, and cut into ¼-inch slices. Place in a salad bowl and set aside.
2. In a skillet, cook the bacon over moderate heat until brown; drain off most of the grease and add the chopped onion. Cook for 5 minutes. Stir in the vinegar, ¼ cup water, the beef stock, salt, and pepper and cook for 1 minute longer.
3. Pour the hot sauce over the potatoes. Gently mix and taste for seasoning. Sprinkle with the chopped parsley just before serving. Serve at once or let stand at room temperature, then serve.

I get most of my recipes from the chefs in Bavaria. They are eager to share their secrets. The best ones are from the housewives—they take the time to prepare a good meal!

SCHWARZWÄLDER KIRSCHTORTE

1 tablespoon shortening
¾ cup flour
10 tablespoons butter
3 eggs, at room temperature
1 teaspoon vanilla extract
1¾ cup sugar
½ cup unsweetened cocoa
¼ cup plus 3 tablespoons kirsch

1 cup drained canned sour cherries
2½ cups whipping cream
⅓ cup confectioners' sugar
1 (4-ounce) bar milk chocolate, at room temperature
1 jar maraschino cherries, drained and rinsed (approximately)

1. Preheat oven to 350°.
2. Grease the sides and bottom of two 9″ round cake pans with the shortening. Sprinkle 2 tablespoons of the flour in each pan and coat sides and bottom well; discard excess.
3. In a small saucepan, melt the butter over low heat. Set aside. Beat the eggs, vanilla extract, and 1 cup of the sugar on high speed of an electric mixer for at least 10 minutes, or until thick, fluffy, and tripled in bulk.
4. Combine the remaining ½ cup of flour and the cocoa and sift a little at a time into the egg mixture, folding gently. Add the melted butter slowly; do not overmix.
5. Pour the batter into the cake pans and bake in preheated oven for 10 to 15 minutes, or until cake springs back when gently touched. Cool in pans for 5 minutes, then turn out on racks to cool further.
6. To prepare the kirsch syrup, combine the remaining ¾ cup sugar with ¾ cup cold water in a saucepan and boil briskly for 5 minutes, stirring constantly. Cool to lukewarm and add ¼ cup of the kirsch.
7. Prick the cakes with a fork. Sprinkle with the syrup and let stand for 5 minutes. Rinse the sour cherries in cold water and pat dry.
8. With chilled bowl and beaters, whip the cream, adding the confectioners' sugar and the remaining 3 tablespoons of kirsch. Shave the chocolate bar into thin curls with a vegetable peeler. Refrigerate until ready to use.
9. To assemble the torte, place one layer in the center of a serving plate. Spread with a ½-inch thick layer of whipped cream and arrange sour cherries on top, leaving a ½-inch rim. Set the second layer on top. Spread entire torte with whipped cream, mounding it in the center. Garnish with the chocolate curls pressed into the whipped cream on sides and top and decorate with the maraschino cherries placed at 2-inch intervals around the rim. Chill until ready to serve.

The Jackson House

Dinner for Six

Consommé Royale

Mousselines of Walleyed Pike in Leek Leaves

Grapefruit Sorbet

Tournedos of Beef, Bordelaise Sauce

Mélange of Vegetables

Vinaigrette Salad with Mushrooms

Lemon Creams in Ramekins

Wines:
With the Mousselines—Field Stone white wine
With the Tournedos—Beaulieu Cabernet Sauvignon,
Private Reserve, 1968
or
Château Margaux, Médoc
With the Lemon Creams—Freemark Abbey Edelwein, 1975

Mary Helen DeLong, Owner

THE JACKSON HOUSE

I t's insane, absolutely," swears Mary Helen DeLong, a sixty-ish mother of eight surveying her newest charge, the Jackson House. "But I'm old enough to be crazy, and anyway— it's done!" The adventurous project, on the drawing boards since 1975, still strikes her as a minor miracle.

In 1884 Charles Jackson built the landmark Jackson House hotel in Anoka, which then thrived with a booming lumber trade. Folks made a half-day horse and buggy pleasure trip from Minneapolis, or a Mississippi riverboat excursion, simply to relax at the Jackson House and dine on its fabled shipped-in blue point oysters or out-of-season strawberries. But the days of lumber glory faded. By the mid-seventies, the town's oldest building had become an eyesore and was destined for destruction until Mary Helen rescued it and returned it to its former handsome state. The historical preservation project became a family affair. Son Marc restored the patterned tin ceilings, recreated the oak portals and pillars of its earlier days, and replaced the Victorian chandeliers and stained-glass windows. Heavy lace curtains and watercolors of local scenes now grace its wainscoted walls above clusters of posy-decked, candlelit tables dressed in green.

"We are able to reach people who want well-prepared food at reasonable prices," Mary Helen states. "It wouldn't be possible for me to have a place that was any different." Although a novice restaurateur, her exemplary cooking has long been the talk of the town. For decades she has taught fine French cuisine around the city—indeed, around the world, as premier assistant to Simca—Simone Beck, France's high priestess of haute cuisine. Mary Helen has molded her kitchen staff to Simca's high standards and creative cooking philosophy. "The recipes are basically hers, but I inject something of my own to suit our local produce. My cooking style is French because that's where the basic idea of good cooking came from, and those basics are still so good—vegetables that are not overcooked, sauces that are not overpowering.

"Basically what we're doing is the fine home cooking of France—*if* you have a good home cook," Mary Helen grins. "It's not elaborate, and it doesn't have to be. We try to keep everything simple: fresh fish, always a lamb dish, fresh spinach. No packages. We don't use anything a second day. The menu depends on the market—local products plus imagination."

214 Jackson Street
Anoka

CONSOMMÉ ROYALE

1 *pound beef bones with marrow, cracked*
3 *pounds veal knuckles, cut in pieces*
  Bones from 1 stewing chicken
3 *pounds lean beef, cut in 1½-inch cubes*
1 *carrot, coarsely chopped*
1 *stalk celery, coarsely chopped*
1 *leek, cut in 2-inch pieces*
1 *onion, peeled and studded with 5 cloves*

1 *teaspoon salt*
1 *teaspoon peppercorns*
3 *sprigs fresh thyme or ½ teaspoon dried thyme leaves*
1 *sprig marjoram or ¼ teaspoon dried marjoram leaves*
4 *parsley sprigs*
1 *French or Turkish bay leaf*
4 *egg whites, lightly beaten*
4 *egg shells, crushed*
  ROYAL CUSTARD (see next page)

1. Preheat oven to 400°.
2. A day in advance, place the beef bones, veal knuckles, and chicken bones in a roasting pan. Brown the bones in preheated oven for 30 minutes. Add the beef cubes and bake 30 minutes longer, turning to brown well on all sides.
3. Remove roasting pan from oven. Place the browned bones and beef cubes with 4 quarts water in a large stockpot. Deglaze the roasting pan over moderate heat with 2 cups water, stirring and scraping the solidified pan juices. Add to stockpot and let stand for ½ hour.
4. Place over moderate heat and slowly bring to a boil. Reduce heat and simmer 3 to 5 hours, removing scum as it gathers on the surface.
5. Add the carrot, celery, leek, and onion with cloves and return to a boil. Add the salt, peppercorns, thyme, marjoram, parsley, and bay leaf. Reduce heat and simmer 1½ to 2 hours. Remove from heat, cool slightly, and strain into a clean pot through a sieve lined with dampened cheesecloth. Refrigerate overnight.

(continued next page)

6. The next day, remove the congealed fat from the surface of the stock. To clarify, stir the egg whites and egg shells into the stock. Gradually bring to a simmer; do not stir, do not allow to boil, and do not disturb the heavy foam that accumulates on the surface. Simmer 15 minutes, cool, and carefully strain through a sieve lined with dampened cheesecloth. Reserve ½ cup consommé for the Royal Custard.
7. Reheat the consommé and ladle into six bowls. Place the Royal Custard cut into decorative shapes on top and serve at once.

I find that the California bay leaves are too medicinal in aroma to use. You may obtain the Turkish and French bay leaves at gourmet food stores and in the gourmet section of a supermarket.

I wish I could cook all the time. To me, that's the epitome of success: cooking everything I want to cook and people enjoying what I prepare.

ROYAL CUSTARD

3 egg yolks	⅛ teaspoon salt
1 egg	Pinch of nutmeg
½ cup consommé (reserved from the CONSOMMÉ ROYALE)	Dash of cayenne pepper

1. Preheat oven to 325°.
2. In a small bowl, combine the egg yolks and the egg and beat lightly. Add the consommé, salt, nutmeg, and cayenne and whisk to blend.
3. Pour into a 1-quart rectangular glass baking dish and set the dish in a larger baking pan. Fill the larger pan with hot water to a depth of 1 inch. Bake in preheated oven approximately 20 minutes, or until center is nearly solid. Remove from oven and allow to cool.
4. Using aspic cutters, cut the custard into decorative shapes; remove with a small, flexible spatula and place on top of the hot consommé.

THE JACKSON HOUSE

MOUSSELINES OF WALLEYED PIKE IN LEEK LEAVES

1¼ pounds walleyed pike fillets	¼ teaspoon thyme
4 large leeks	½ cup dry white wine
1 carrot, chopped	(approximately)
1 stalk celery, chopped	2 egg yolks
½ small onion, chopped,	1 cup whipping cream
or the tough green	Pinch of grated nutmeg
ends of the leeks	4 drops Tabasco sauce
Salt	3 tablespoons butter
Pepper	FISH SAUCE
	(see next page)

1. Trim the skin and remove the bones from the fillets; reserve. Cut the fillets in 1-inch chunks and chill well.

2. Bring a large pot of water to a rapid boil. Wash the leeks thoroughly; trim the tough green ends. Set aside and reserve the ends if intending to use in the fish stock. Carefully remove twelve of the largest outer leaves. Drop the leaves into the boiling water for about 2 minutes. Immediately drain and refresh in ice water; pat dry and chill.

3. To make the fish stock, place the reserved fish bones and trimmings in a casserole. Add the carrot, celery, onion or green leek ends, ¼ teaspoon salt, ¼ teaspoon pepper, a pinch of the thyme, and the wine. Bring to a boil and cook for 1 minute. Add enough water to cover and return to a boil; reduce heat and simmer 25 minutes. Strain and set aside. Chill 3 tablespoons of stock for use in the Fish Sauce.

4. Place the chilled fish chunks in a food processor. While processing, gradually add the egg yolks, cream, nutmeg, Tabasco, ¼ teaspoon salt, pinch of thyme, and ¼ teaspoon pepper. Process for 2 to 3 minutes, or until mixture is homogenized and the consistency of mousse.

5. Preheat oven to 325°. Grease a 14-inch by 8-inch baking dish with 1 tablespoon of the butter.

(continued next page)

6. Lay the chilled leek leaves on a flat surface. Neatly trim ends to make a rectangle. Place about 2 tablespoons of the fish mousse near the base of each leaf. Roll up to enclose the mousse filling compactly.

7. Arrange rolls seam side down in the baking dish. Dot rolls with the remaining 2 tablespoons butter. Pour 5 tablespoons of the stock over the rolls. Bring to a simmer over moderate heat. Immediately remove from heat and cover tightly with parchment and aluminum foil; bake in preheated oven 15 minutes. Remove and serve two rolls each on six warmed dinner plates. Sprinkle with pepper to taste. Dress the rolls with a little of the Fish Sauce and pass the remaining sauce in a sauceboat.

FISH SAUCE

¾ cup butter
3 tablespoons fresh lemon
  juice
3 tablespoons fish stock
  (reserved from
  Mousselines of
  Walleyed Pike)

3 egg yolks
Salt
Cayenne pepper

1. Melt the butter and remove from heat.

2. Combine the lemon juice with the fish stock. In a heavy saucepan, place the egg yolks and 3 tablespoons of the lemon juice/fish stock mixture. Cook over moderate heat, whisking constantly, until the yolks are just beginning to scramble. Remove and immediately add the remaining 3 tablespoons liquid.

3. Whisk the melted butter into the egg mixture, a little at a time. Beat until very smooth and somewhat thickened. Add salt and cayenne to taste. Serve at once with the Mousselines of Walleyed Pike.

The most difficult thing in preparing this sauce is to learn how to taste. The sauce must taste the same every time. Dried herbs can be a big problem—they're different every time you use them, so you must keep your taste goal in mind.

THE JACKSON HOUSE

GRAPEFRUIT SORBET

¾ cup superfine sugar   1 cup grapefruit juice
                                            with pulp

1. Chill six wine glasses.
2. In a saucepan, bring the sugar and 1 cup water to a boil and cook about 1 minute until the sugar is dissolved. Let cool.
3. Stir the syrup and juice together until well combined, then pour into the container of an ice cream freezer and freeze, following directions on the machine, until firm.
4. Serve in the well-chilled glasses following the fish course to refresh the palate for the meat course.

Note: It is not necessary to strain the pulp from the juice.

TOURNEDOS OF BEEF, BORDELAISE SAUCE

¾ cup good-quality dry
   red wine
1½ tablespoons minced shallots
¾ cup canned beef bouillon
   (preferably Crosse and
   Blackwell)
6 (6-ounce) filets of beef
   tenderloin

½ cup salad oil
   (approximately)
½ pound butter
   (approximately)
   Salt and pepper
¼ pound beef marrow

1. In a heavy saucepan, place the wine, shallots, and beef bouillon and cook about 15 minutes until the liquid is reduced by half. Lightly oil the filets on each side with about 3 tablespoons of the oil.

2. In a heavy skillet, heat 2 tablespoons of the oil with about ¼ pound of the butter. When hot, cook three of the filets until medium rare by frying 4 minutes on one side and 3 minutes on the other. Remove from skillet; place on a warmed plate and keep warm in a low oven. Repeat with the remaining three filets, 2 tablespoons oil, and ¼ pound butter.

3. Deglaze the skillet with the reduced wine/beef bouillon mixture, stirring and scraping the small browned bits; correct seasoning with salt and pepper.

4. At the same time, bring salted water to a boil in a small saucepan. Remove pan from heat and add the marrow. Let stand 5 minutes. Remove the marrow from water and dice half of it; add the diced portion to the sauce in the skillet.

5. Reheat the sauce and cook until hot and the marrow is half melted. Place the filets on six warmed plates. Pour the sauce over and lay a slice of the remaining marrow on each serving. Serve at once with the Mélange of Vegetables.

We try to use the best American ingredients with the care and precision of the French. That's their claim to fame, and it's stood the test of time.

MÉLANGE OF VEGETABLES

4 small carrots, peeled
and cut into julienne
strips
5 tablespoons butter
1 (1-inch) piece gingerroot,
peeled

Salt
3 to 4 grinds fresh pepper
18 small broccoli florets
1 cup fresh peas
2 tablespoons minced parsley

1. In a small casserole which will hold the carrots without crowding, place the carrots, 3 tablespoons of the butter, gingerroot, ½ teaspoon salt, and pepper. Cover the carrots with cold water. Bring to a boil and simmer until crisp-tender, about 3 to 4 minutes. Set aside.
2. Pour 1 quart water each into two separate pots and bring to a boil. Place the broccoli in one pot, the peas in the other. When water returns to a boil, add ¼ teaspoon salt to each. Cook until crisp-tender, about 2 minutes; drain thoroughly.
3. Drain the carrots, reserving the broth. Strain, then pour the broth into a saucepan and add the remaining 2 tablespoons butter; reduce about 1 minute until there is no water remaining in the seasoned butter.
4. Toss all the vegetables separately in the seasoned butter and arrange attractively either on individual serving plates or one large serving platter. Garnish with the minced parsley.

We believe in adapting the cooking techniques of France to utilize the best of our own local produce. Other seasonal vegetables—asparagus, celery root, whatever produces a contrast of taste and texture—can be substituted.

THE JACKSON HOUSE

VINAIGRETTE SALAD WITH MUSHROOMS

1 head romaine lettuce
½ pound mushrooms
¼ cup wine vinegar
1 teaspoon salt
¼ teaspoon freshly ground
pepper

1 teaspoon finely minced
fresh tarragon
1 teaspoon finely minced
shallots
1 cup salad oil

1. Rinse the romaine, pat dry, and tear into bite-size segments. Wash the mushrooms, wipe dry, and slice.
2. Assemble the romaine in one large or six individual salad bowls. Top with the mushrooms.
3. Combine the vinegar, salt, pepper, tarragon, and shallots in a small bowl and allow to macerate 10 to 30 minutes. Whisk in the oil in a thin stream and continue to whisk until thoroughly incorporated. Just before serving, drizzle over the salad and toss lightly to coat evenly.

Following the lessons learned abroad with Simone Beck, I prefer to use either French virgin olive oil or French peanut oil.

THE JACKSON HOUSE

LEMON CREAMS IN RAMEKINS

3 tablespoons butter
(approximately)
Zest of 2 lemons,
finely grated
⅓ cup lemon juice

5 egg yolks
⅔ cup sugar
3 egg whites
Pinch of salt
Confectioners' sugar

1. Generously grease six ½-cup porcelain or glass ramekins with about 1 tablespoon of the butter. Place the grated lemon zest, lemon juice, egg yolks, remaining 2 tablespoons butter, and ⅓ cup of the sugar in a small, heavy saucepan. Whisk over low heat until the mixture is hot to the fingers and thickens slightly; it should not boil.
2. Remove the pan from the heat and whisk for 1 to 2 minutes to cool the mixture and keep it from scrambling on the bottom.
3. Preheat oven to 250°.
4. Beat the egg whites with the salt until they form soft peaks. Sprinkle on the remaining ⅓ cup sugar and continue beating until the whites form fairly stiff and shiny peaks. Delicately fold into the warm lemon mixture. Pour into the ramekins and bake in preheated oven for 25 minutes. Serve warm or cold in the molds sprinkled with confectioners' sugar.

It is essential that the ramekins cook in a very slow oven.

Dinner for Six

French Onion Soup

Green Salad with Sour Cream Dressing

Standing Prime Rib Roast

Yorkshire Pudding

Stuffed Tomato

Baked Apples

Wine:

Cabernet Sauvignon

Bill Kozlak, Proprietor

Kenneth Wolf, Executive Chef

JAX CAFE

In 1910 Stan Kozlak erected a brick building to house his various businesses. It was converted to Jax Cafe in 1933—the moment prohibition ended—and its grand mahogany bar has been a monument to northeast Minneapolis's hospitality every since.

Joe Kozlak, the eldest of Stan's five boys, expanded the business in 1943 as his own family expanded. Today it is managed by Joe's son Bill, born just a block away and recruited early on to help his mother and brothers in the kitchen. Today Bill's practiced eye roves the series of comfortable wood-paneled dining rooms and the garden patio beyond with its slowly turning millwheel, waterfall, and trout stream, where guests can net their own dinners and pose for photos on its grassy banks.

The fish come fresh from the Kozlak's rural Minnesota trout farm. Other seafood, including the lobsters that sport in the bar's aquarium, are flown in with regularity. Minnesota walleyed pike is nearly as popular as the aged and cut-to-order tenderloins and New York strips upon which Jax has staked its reputation and which, as Bill notes, prove to be quite a competition: "You're in mid-America; beef's the big seller." Nevertheless, also popular are the house chowder, clams casino, and creamy Caesar salad, not to mention the Viennese dinners that Kozlak throws whenever the spirit moves him or whenever the customers insist. They come—sixteen busloads at a time—for the weekend football lunches which are "a tradition. It's the thing to do."

It is a place for celebrations of all kinds. Kids which Bill once lifted into highchairs are now returning with kids of their own. Birthday cakes appear with regularity from the kitchen, with a few more candles as the years go by. Couples celebrate their fiftieth anniversaries here in the hall where they held their wedding dances. "Lots of people get engaged at these tables and come back to get married in the patio," says Bill, as he sends a complimentary bottle of champagne to the newlyweds holding hands at the window table.

The numerous framed awards on the restaurant's walls are bronze testimonials to Jax's good food. Even more treasured is the longstanding place of honor that it holds in its patrons' hearts. Bill's Minnesotan philosophy sums it up: "Treat your customers like friends you have invited into your home."

1928 University Avenue N.E.
Minneapolis

JAX CAFE

FRENCH ONION SOUP

2 chicken bouillon cubes	3 tablespoons flour
2 beef bouillon cubes	¼ cup sherry
4 large onions, peeled and halved	6 slices French bread
4 tablespoons butter	½ cup grated Parmesan cheese (approximately)

1. In a large saucepan, bring 1½ quarts water to boil and dissolve the chicken and beef bouillon cubes. Reduce heat.
2. Thinly slice the onions and separate the rings. In a sauté pan placed over very low heat, slowly sauté the onion rings in the butter, stirring with a wooden spoon until they become transparent and barely amber.
3. Sprinkle the flour over the onions and stir until blended. While continuing to stir, add the sherry and simmer 3 minutes.
4. Add the onion mixture to the bouillon; bring to a boil, stirring constantly. Immediately reduce heat and simmer 20 minutes.
5. Toast the French bread slices and sprinkle them with grated Parmesan cheese. Ladle the hot soup into six warmed bowls and float one slice over each. Serve at once.

GREEN SALAD WITH SOUR CREAM DRESSING

6 small heads Bibb lettuce or 3 heads romaine	2 tablespoons grated onion or 1 clove garlic, minced
6 hard-cooked eggs, chopped	Pinch of cayenne pepper
1 cup sour cream	Salt
2 tablespoons lemon juice	

1. Wash the lettuce in cold water, separate the leaves and pat dry. Tear the leaves into smaller pieces; chill.
2. Divide the lettuce leaves between six chilled salad bowls. Sprinkle the chopped eggs evenly over.
3. Combine the sour cream, lemon juice, onion or garlic, and cayenne; season to taste with the salt. Just before serving, pour the dressing over the lettuce.

JAX CAFE

STANDING PRIME RIB ROAST

½ pound butter
1 (6-rib) standing beef roast,
    at room temperature
    (about 10 pounds)

Salt and pepper
Lawry's seasoned salt
HORSERADISH SAUCE

1. Preheat oven to 450°.
2. Melt the butter in a saucepan over low heat. Place the roast, fat and round side up, in a shallow roasting pan. Rub entire surface with salt, pepper, and seasoned salt to taste. Brush on the melted butter.
3. Roast in preheated oven 20 minutes.
4. Add 1 cup water to bottom of pan. Reduce temperature to 350° and roast 1¾ to 2 hours longer for a rare roast, or until a meat thermometer registers 130°. Remove from oven and reserve ¼ cup of the hot drippings for the Yorkshire Pudding. Loosely cover the roast with aluminum foil and let stand 15 to 20 minutes.
5. To carve, stand the roast on its wide flat side and slice horizontally across the grain then down along the rib bone; allow one slice per person. Place the slices on six warmed plates. Drizzle the remaining pan drippings over each and serve with the Horseradish Sauce. Accompany with the Yorkshire Pudding and Stuffed Tomato.

Note: Adjust the roasting time (step 4) to 15 minutes per pound for a medium-rare roast, 18 minutes per pound for one well done.

Instruct the butcher to cut the roast so that it will be easy to carve.

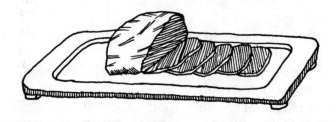

JAX CAFE

HORSERADISH SAUCE

½ cup grated fresh
    horseradish
¼ cup sour cream

1 tablespoon Worcestershire
    sauce
Pinch of salt

Combine all ingredients and let stand at least 1 hour to allow flavors to blend. Serve as a condiment with the Standing Prime Rib Roast.

The horseradish sauce is very expensive for us to offer, but customers love it.

YORKSHIRE PUDDING

1 cup flour
4 eggs, at room temperature
1 cup milk, at room
    temperature
Pinch of ground nutmeg

Salt
¼ cup hot pan drippings
    (reserved from the
    Standing Rib Roast)

1. Preheat oven to 375°.
2. Mix the flour and the eggs thoroughly. Add the milk and nutmeg and season with the salt; beat together well.
3. Heat two six-cup muffin tins. Generously grease the tins with the hot pan drippings. Pour the pudding batter into the tins until three-fourths full. Bake in preheated oven for 45 minutes. Do not open oven door during baking; cold air may cause the pudding to fall. Remove and serve at once.

JAX CAFE

STUFFED TOMATO

4 tablespoons butter
6 medium-size firm
   tomatoes

2 cups fresh peas
½ cup grated Parmesan
   cheese

1. Preheat oven to 375°. Melt the butter in a small pan.
2. With a sharp knife, slice off the top from each tomato ¼ inch from the stem. Hollow out the seeds and juice and invert on a rack to drain.
3. Bring water to a rapid boil in a saucepan. Parboil the peas for 3 to 4 minutes; remove from heat and drain. Fill the tomatoes with the peas, then sprinkle the tops with the Parmesan cheese. Drizzle the butter over each and bake in preheated oven 15 minutes. Serve at once.

Note: Frozen peas may be substituted for the fresh.

JAX CAFE

BAKED APPLES

½ cup corn syrup
½ cup sugar
½ cup orange marmalade
4 tablespoons butter
6 baking apples (preferably Rome Beauty)

½ cup brown sugar
3 tablespoons raisins
½ teaspoon cinnamon
1 quart vanilla ice cream

1. Preheat oven to 325°.
2. In a small saucepan, combine the syrup, sugar, marmalade, and butter. Cook gently over medium heat, stirring until sugar is dissolved. Pour into baking pan.
3. Wash and core the apples; peel about 1 inch from the top.
4. In a small bowl, combine the brown sugar, raisins, and cinnamon. Fill the apples with the brown sugar mixture and place peeled side down in the baking pan. Cover and bake 30 minutes. Turn over and baste with the syrup in the pan. Bake, uncovered, 15 minutes longer. Remove and serve on dessert plates with scoops of the vanilla ice cream.

People might be watching their calories at lunch, but at night now they're looking for desserts.

KIKUGAWA

Dinner for Six

Negimaki

Otoshi

Chawan Mushi

Sashimi

Salmon Teriyaki

Beef Teriyaki

Shrimp and Vegetable Tempura

Sunomono Salad

Beverages:
With the Appetizers—Numano saké, served hot
With the Entrées—Numano Koshu plum wine or Kirin beer
After dinner—tea

John Omori, Principal Owner
Kazutoshi Sogabe, Manager
Chikashi Todoroki, Chef

KIKUGAWA

Kikugawa restaurant, whose name means "river of chrysan-
themums," is a modern shrine to age-old Japanese cuisine and
culture. The dream-come-true of manager John Omori, whose
first home was on the shores of the Kikugawa, its serenity is the understated ideal of master Japanese artists.

This new restaurant on the skyway level of the Pillsbury Center is an
arcade of clear glass that overlooks the building's many-angled atrium
and the open-air plaza across the avenue. Transparent aquariums,
polished ash-blond curves of wood, and deep tones of mahogany and
plum form the backdrop for the sleek design that melds the contemporary with the past. An angled room holds a tiny sushi bar with a
panoply of seafood morsels displayed in lacquered serving boxes.
Stretching beyond are tables outfitted with cooking burners and a
tatami area for traditional cushioned seating.

"The chrysanthemum is the traditional symbol of the Japanese Imperial
court," John advises, "and we serve our guests with traditional hospitality." Japanese-born servers, clothed in obis and kimonos, provide
the preliminary warm towel refresher, followed by a multiplicity of
dainty courses. "The whole meal is an appetizer. You just keep on eating and drinking." Under the direction of a Tokyo-trained head chef,
Kikugawa's cuisine is characterized by lightness, delicacy, and simplicity. "We try to preserve the natural flavors," points out the manager.
"Instead of mincing, puréeing or seasoning ingredients into oblivion,
the food's intrinsic color, shape, and texture are given equal billing
with taste.

"Even the fresh raw garnishes are designed to represent nature—
birds and flowers, never an artificial form." This dedication to artistry is
no less apparent in the extensive variety of cooking styles which make
up Kikugawa's many-course gourmet dinners: uncooked sushi and
sashimi, sukiyaki, teriyaki, fondue-style shabu-shabu, deep-fried ten-
drils of tempura, with curls of pickled ginger always available for
cleansing the palate. For dessert in Japanese fashion, Kikugawa offers
pungent pickles and rice. For those who crave a touch of sweet, John
recommends flavored ices or sweet red beans which "may not sound
too good," he smilingly admits, "but which really are!"

Pillsbury Center
200 South 6th Street
Minneapolis

KIKUGAWA

In a formal Japanese dinner called kaiseki ryōri, *the Negimaki, Otoshi, Chawan Mushi, and Sashimi are served in consecutive order before the featured teriyaki and tempura dishes.*

NEGIMAKI
Beef Roll

½ cup Japanese soy sauce
½ cup mirin
2 tablespoons sugar

¾ pound New York strip
   beef, sliced paper thin
1 bunch green onions

1. Preheat broiler. To make a basting sauce, combine the soy sauce, mirin, and sugar. Set aside.
2. Cut the beef slices into 6-inch by 2-inch strips. Wash and trim the green onions. Cut into 2-inch pieces. Place several pieces at the base of each beef strip and roll tightly. Secure with toothpicks.
3. Lay the rolls on a broiler rack; baste generously with the sauce. Place under preheated broiler and broil about 2 minutes, basting again after the first minute. The beef should be tender but not overcooked.
4. Remove from broiler; cool slightly and take out toothpicks. Cut each roll in two and serve on a plate.

Mirin is a Japanese sweet rice wine used for cooking. If it is unavailable, substitute with a mixture of one part sugar to two parts sherry.

Japanese cuisine emphasizes the natural flavor of fresh ingredients, even when food is broiled.

We usually have several appetizers, some cold, some hot. In Japan, the cold ones are the most popular.

OTOSHI
Fish Balls

2 cups vegetable oil
   (approximately)
5 mushrooms, finely chopped
1 carrot, finely chopped
¾ pound ground cod

1 egg
½ cup cornstarch
   (approximately)
Salt
Dash of saké

1. Heat the oil in a skillet until sizzling hot (360°).
2. Combine the mushrooms, carrot, cod, egg, and the cornstarch to bind. Season to taste with salt and add the saké. Shape into 1-inch balls and deep-fry in the hot oil about 3 minutes until done. Remove with slotted spoon and drain. Arrange on a platter and serve hot.

In Japan, the traditional foods never change; here our service is also traditional, starting with a hot towel.

CHAWAN MUSHI
Steamed Egg Custard

6 small fresh shrimp, shelled
   and deveined
6 scallops
½ chicken breast, skinned
5 mushrooms, finely chopped
2 bamboo shoots, finely
   chopped

Salt
4 cups dashi, at room
   temperature (preferably
   Nomoto brand)
3 eggs, beaten

1. Preheat oven to 350°.
2. Parboil the shrimp and the scallops about 30 seconds. Cut the chicken and the parboiled shrimp and scallops into ¼-inch pieces. Lightly season the mushrooms and bamboo shoots with salt. Set aside.
3. Gradually drizzle the dashi into the beaten eggs; mix slightly but do not beat. Strain.

4. Place equal portions of the shrimp, scallops, chicken, mushrooms, and bamboo shoots in six custard cups. Add the custard mixture. Place in a baking pan filled with water to a level of 1 inch. Steam in preheated oven for 25 minutes. Serve warm.

Instant dashi, a variation of the basic soup stock made from dried bonito shavings, is available at Japanese food markets.

SASHIMI
Raw Fish Fillet

1 *pound fresh tuna, cut in sashimi fillets*	*Wasabi*
¾ *pound fresh halibut, cut in sashimi fillets*	1 *cup Japanese soy sauce*

1. Using a very sharp knife, slice the fillets into 2-inch strips. Cut the strips ⅛-inch thick to form a row of rectangular or domino-shaped slices. Layer the slices on a chilled serving dish. Set aside.
2. Mix about ⅛ teaspoon of the wasabi with the soy sauce. Taste and add more wasabi, if desired; place in saucers for dipping. Serve with the sashimi.

Note: Wasabi, a stinging hot, green horseradish root, is virtually impossible to find in the United States. It is available in Oriental markets, however, in tubes of paste or tins of powder. To reconstitute the powder, put about a teaspoon of powder in a bowl and add a little tepid water. Add more powder or water as needed to form a thick paste. Mix until smooth, cover, and let stand about 10 minutes.

Wasabi grows like gingerroot. In Japan if it's fresh, that's a first class restaurant, but that's rare to find. A powdered form will work.

Use the freshest fish available. Cut it sharply and take care to display it neatly on the dish.

KIKUGAWA

SALMON TERIYAKI

3 cups Japanese soy sauce
3 cups mirin
3 tablespoons sugar

3 pounds fresh salmon
Oil

1. Combine the soy sauce, mirin, and sugar. Slice the salmon into six 8-ounce steaks. Marinate in the soy sauce/mirin mixture about 4 hours.
2. Preheat broiler.
3. Remove the steaks from the marinade and pat dry. Lightly oil a broiler pan; arrange the steaks on the pan. Broil on both sides 5 to 6 minutes. Remove and arrange on an attractive platter. Serve at once.

The salmon and tuna here are better than any in Japan. We've been lucky in locating good supplies.

KIKUGAWA

BEEF TERIYAKI

3 cups Japanese soy sauce
3 cups mirin
3 tablespoons sugar

Oil
6 (7-ounce) New York
 strip steaks

1. To make a basting sauce, combine the soy sauce, mirin, and sugar. Set aside.
2. Preheat broiler.
3. Lightly oil a broiler pan and arrange the steaks on the pan. Using a pastry brush, baste the steaks generously with the sauce and broil 4 inches from heat about 2 minutes. Baste again and broil 2 to 3 minutes longer. Baste once more and turn carefully. Repeat for other side. Remove the steaks to a platter and keep warm.
4. Stir the pan juices over high heat with remaining basting sauce. Coat the steaks in this sauce about ½ minute on each side to glaze. Place the steaks on six plates and drizzle a little sauce over each. Serve at once.

In Japan there are tremendous differences in seasoning but not in style of cooking. In Tokyo it's heavier, and in Kyoto lighter. Ours is done more in the Tokyo style, cooked in stronger soy sauce.

KIKUGAWA

SHRIMP AND VEGETABLE TEMPURA

12 medium-size fresh shrimp	Vegetable oil
6 fresh spears asparagus	1 cup flour
1 small (4" to 5" long) eggplant	1 egg yolk
	Ice cubes
½ yellow summer squash	Japanese soy sauce

1. Place a metal bowl and 1 cup water in the refrigerator to chill.
2. Shell and devein the shrimp, leaving the tails intact. Cut each shrimp down the back so that it lies flat and forms a butterfly. Arrange on a plate, cover with plastic wrap, and refrigerate until time to use.
3. Cut the asparagus spears in 2-inch sections. Cut the stem off the eggplant and slice in half across the middle, then slice each half lengthwise in ½-inch sections. Cut the squash in ¼-inch rounds. Arrange the vegetables neatly on a tray and set aside.
4. Heat the oil in a deep-fryer to 350°.
5. Place the flour in the well-chilled metal bowl. In a separate bowl, beat the egg yolk slightly and add the chilled water and ice cubes. Beat a few strokes, then combine loosely with the flour. Do not over-mix; the batter should be lumpy.
6. Set the foods, batter, a rack or paper towels for draining, and a slotted spoon near the hot oil. Coat the vegetables and the shrimp in the batter, a few pieces at a time, slide into the oil, and deep-fry about 3 minutes, or until golden. Do not overfry. Arrange attractively on a serving platter, and serve hot with small saucers of soy sauce for dipping.

Dip the tempura delicately into the soy sauce. Vegetables should be only lightly seasoned. Be sure not to cover them with too much sauce.

KIKUGAWA

SUNOMONO SALAD

3 cucumbers
1 tablespoon vinegar
1 tablespoon sugar

Salt
¾ pound lump crabmeat

1. Cut the cucumbers into halves and remove seeds; cut in thin slices. Set aside.
2. Mix the vinegar, sugar, 2½ tablespoons water, and salt to taste.
3. Marinate the cucumber slices and the crabmeat in the sauce for ½ hour. Serve in small bowls at room temperature.

This salad is pure Japanese: I don't serve anything which you won't find in Japan.

It's very Japanese to have rice only at the end of a meal. That's all we eat of rice. If you wish to finish with something sweet, serve ice cream or sherbet.

Leeann Chin

Dinner for Six

Hot and Sour Soup

Egg Rolls

Lemon Chicken

Mixed Vegetable Stir-Fry

Almond Cookies

Wine:

Wan Fu

Leeann Chin, Proprietor and Chef

LEEANN CHIN

T he word *popular* greatly understates Leeann Chin's Chinese cuisine. "They telephone from all over—New York, Seattle, and San Francisco," proprietor and chef Leeann modestly beams. "First they make a dinner reservation, then they buy a plane ticket."

The success of this restaurant is clearly due to Leeann, for whom food has always been a way of life. In her native Canton her father owned a restaurant and later a grocery store. "All we talked about at meals was the food we were eating," she recalls. The husband she married in Hong King was no different: "He was really fussy about Chinese food; he never let a meal go by without finding some little thing wrong—and not too many compliments. I like my compliments, so I worked hard to improve." Her five children thrived on the results, but it was not until 1972 that others were introduced to her Cantonese cuisine.

She operated at that time a modest sewing business in downtown Minneapolis. To thank her clients for their gifts and patronage, she would invite them home for lunch. Her guests raved about the meals and persuaded her to begin cooking classes. Catering soon followed, which was "a good learning process." Bowing to demands that she go public with this fare, in 1980 she cautiously sought a location suited to her high standards. She settled upon a space in Bonaventure, Minnetonka's aristocratic shopping mall, where understated luxury makes a tasteful statement. The restaurant was made as chic as its locale, with walls that eschew harsh angles and instead seem to undulate in curves of sandy beige. Matching banquettes and blond birch chairs cluster around glassed pedestals that house treasures of Chinese ivory. Each table's slim marble vase bears a single silken iris. The room's serenity is spiced by a splash of contemporary Oriental prints on the wall and a backdrop of glass that mirrors the room's raison d'être, Leeann's buffet of appetizers and entrées.

"Cantonese food is healthier and has more variety than other Chinese food," Leeann says about her native cuisine, "and it's fun to cook many different things; that's why I like my buffet style of serving. That way I can introduce people to so many new dishes. Everybody's plate is clean when they leave—and that's a higher compliment than anything else."

Bonaventure Mall
Highway 12 & Plymouth Road
Minnetonka

LEEANN CHIN

HOT AND SOUR SOUP

6 medium-size dried black mushrooms	3 tablespoons white vinegar
¼ pound boneless pork loin	½ cup shredded canned bamboo shoots
2½ teaspoons cornstarch	¼ teaspoon white pepper
1½ teaspoons salt	2 eggs, slightly beaten
1 tablespoon plus ½ teaspoon soy sauce	2 tablespoons chopped green onions (with tops)
6 ounces bean curd	2 teaspoons red pepper sauce
4 cups canned chicken broth	½ teaspoon sesame oil

1. Soak the mushrooms in warm water to cover until soft, approximately 30 minutes; drain. Rinse in warm water; drain. Remove and discard stems. Cut caps into thin slices.

2. Trim fat from the pork. Shred the pork into ⅛-inch slices, cutting against the grain. Place in a glass or plastic bowl and toss with ½ teaspoon of the cornstarch, ½ teaspoon of the salt, and the ½ teaspoon soy sauce. Cover and refrigerate for 15 minutes. Cut the bean curd into 1½-inch by 1¼-inch pieces.

3. In a 3-quart saucepan, heat the chicken broth, vinegar, the remaining 1 tablespoon soy sauce, and the remaining 1 teaspoon salt until boiling. Stir in the bamboo shoots, mushrooms, seasoned pork, and bean curd. Heat to boiling; reduce heat to low. Cover and simmer 5 minutes.

4. Mix the remaining 2 tablespoons cornstarch, 2 tablespoons cold water, and white pepper; stir into soup. Heat to boiling, stirring constantly. Pour the beaten eggs slowly into the soup, stirring constantly with a fork until the egg forms cooked shreds. Stir in the green onions, red pepper sauce, and sesame oil. Serve hot in individual bowls.

For a Chinese meal, it is a good idea to have several dishes that can be started or completed ahead of time. This hot and sour soup is just such a do-ahead dish, if you wish, and goes well with most Chinese menus.

EGG ROLLS

5 medium-size dried
black mushrooms
½ pound ground pork
1½ teaspoons salt
½ teaspoon cornstarch
½ teaspoon soy sauce
Dash of white pepper
1 (2½-pound) green
cabbage, finely shredded
2 cups vegetable oil
(approximately)
¼ cup shredded canned
bamboo shoots

½ pound cooked shrimp,
finely chopped
⅓ cup finely chopped
green onions (with tops)
1 teaspoon five-spice powder
1 (1-pound) package egg
roll skins
1 egg, beaten
¼ cup hot dry mustard
RED SWEET AND SOUR
SAUCE

1. Soak the mushrooms in warm water until soft, approximately 30 minutes; drain. Rinse in warm water; drain. Remove and discard stems. Cut caps into thin strips. Set aside. Mix pork, ½ teaspoon of the salt, the cornstarch, soy sauce, and pepper. Cover and refrigerate approximately 20 minutes.

2. Heat 2 quarts water to boiling in Dutch oven; add the cabbage. Heat again to boiling; cover and cook 1 minute; drain. Rinse with cold water until cabbage is cold. Drain thoroughly; remove excess water by squeezing cabbage.

3. Heat wok until 2 drops water bubble and skitter when sprinkled in the wok. Add 2 tablespoons of the oil and rotate to coat sides. Add the seasoned pork; stir-fry until pork is no longer pink. Add the mushrooms and bamboo shoots; stir-fry 1 minute. Stir in the cabbage, shrimp, green onions, remaining 1 teaspoon salt, and the five-spice powder; cool.

4. Place ½ cup of the egg roll filling slightly below the center of an egg roll skin. Cover the remaining skins with a dampened towel to keep them pliable. Fold the corner of skin closest to filling over, tucking the point under the filling. Fold in and overlap the two opposite corners. Brush fourth corner with egg and roll up to seal. Repeat with remaining skins. Cover the filled rolls with a dampened towel or plastic wrap to prevent drying out.

5. Pour the remaining oil in a wok to a depth of 2 inches and heat to 350°. Fry four or five rolls at a time for 2 to 3 minutes until golden brown, turning three times. Drain on paper towel and keep hot.

6. Meanwhile, stir the mustard with 3 tablespoons plus 1½ teaspoons cold water until smooth. Let stand 5 minutes before serving. Serve the egg rolls with the hot mustard and Red Sweet and Sour Sauce.

RED SWEET AND SOUR SAUCE

½ cup red wine vinegar	⅓ cup sugar
½ cup catsup	15 drops red pepper sauce

Mix all ingredients in a small bowl. Serve immediately or make in advance, cover, and refrigerate.

My recipes are based on what I saw and what I ate growing up in my father's restaurant in Canton. Of course, they can be adapted to American tastes and ways.

LEMON CHICKEN

2 whole chicken breasts
(approximately 2 pounds)
Oil
1 egg
3 tablespoons plus 2
teaspoons cornstarch
1¾ teaspoons salt
1 teaspoon soy sauce
White pepper
¼ cup flour
¼ teaspoon baking soda

½ cup canned chicken broth
¼ cup honey
3 tablespoons lemon juice
2 tablespoons light
corn syrup
2 tablespoons vinegar
1 tablespoon catsup
1 clove garlic, minced
Peel of ½ lemon
½ lemon, thinly sliced

1. Remove bones and skin from the chicken breasts and discard. Cut each breast into fourths. Place in a shallow glass or plastic dish.

2. Mix 1 tablespoon oil, the egg, 2 teaspoons cornstarch, 1 teaspoon of the salt, the soy sauce, and ¼ teaspoon white pepper; pour over the chicken. Turn chicken to coat both sides. Cover and refrigerate 30 minutes. Remove chicken from marinade and reserve marinade.

3. Pour oil into wok to a depth of 1½ inches and heat to 350°. Mix the reserved marinade, the flour, ¼ cup water, 2 tablespoons of the cornstarch, 2 tablespoons oil, the baking soda, and ¼ teaspoon of the salt. Dip the chicken pieces one at a time into this batter. Fry two pieces at a time for 3 minutes or until light brown. Drain on paper towel.

4. Increase oil temperature to 375°. Return chicken to wok and fry together approximately 2 minutes, until golden brown, turning once. Drain on paper towel. Cut each piece crosswise into five to six pieces. Place in single layer on a heated platter and keep warm.

5. To make sauce, heat the chicken broth, honey, lemon juice, corn syrup, vinegar, 1 tablespoon oil, catsup, garlic, the remaining ½ teaspoon salt, dash of white pepper, and the lemon peel to boiling. Mix the remaining 1 tablespoon cornstarch with 1 tablespoon cold water and stir into sauce. Cook and stir until thickened, approximately 10 seconds. Remove lemon peel. Pour the sauce over the chicken and garnish with the lemon slices. Serve at once.

Note: The chicken can be prepared one day in advance through step 3. The sauce, also, can be prepared then covered and stored in the refrigerator up to twenty-four hours. Reheat the sauce to boiling when ready to serve.

Friends began to ask me to plan their dinner parties. "I don't want to have anything to do with it," they'd say. "Whatever you plan will be wonderful!"

MIXED VEGETABLE STIR-FRY

1 pound bok choy or 4
  large celery stalks
½ pound pea pods
½ pound mushrooms
4 green onions (with tops)
2 tablespoons cornstarch
½ cup vegetable oil
4 thin slices gingerroot,
  finely chopped

2 cloves garlic, finely
  chopped
1 cup sliced, canned
  bamboo shoots
1 cup canned chicken broth,
  or water
2 teaspoons salt
¼ cup oyster sauce

1. Cut the bok choy with its leaves diagonally into ½-inch slices. Snap off ends and remove strings from the pea pods. Place the pea pods in boiling water to cover and cook, covered, 1 minute; drain. Immediately rinse under cold water and drain again. Cut the mushrooms into ¼-inch slices. Cut the green onions into 2-inch pieces. Mix the cornstarch with 2 tablespoons cold water to dissolve. Set aside.

2. Heat wok until a drop of water bubbles and skitters when sprinkled in the wok. Add the oil and rotate wok to coat sides. Add the gingerroot and garlic; stir-fry until garlic is light brown. Add the bok choy; stir-fry 1 minute. Add the mushrooms and bamboo shoots; stir 1 minute. Stir in the chicken broth and salt; heat to boiling. Stir in the dissolved cornstarch. Cook and stir until thickened, approximately 10 seconds. Add the pea pods, green onions, and oyster sauce. Cook and stir 30 seconds. Serve immediately.

The trick in serving Chinese food to guests, if you don't have much help in the kitchen, is not to plan too many stir-fry dishes because they must be done at the last minute.

LEEANN CHIN

ALMOND COOKIES

1 cup lard
1 cup sugar
2 eggs
2 cups flour
½ teaspoon baking soda

5 drops yellow food coloring
1 teaspoon almond extract
5 dozen whole blanched
 almonds

1. Preheat oven to 350°. Lightly grease two baking sheets.
2. In mixing bowl, beat the lard with the sugar until fluffy. Beat in 1 of the eggs. Add the flour and baking soda, stirring just until blended. Add the food coloring and extract, stirring until blended. Cover tightly with plastic wrap and chill slightly, approximately ½ hour.
3. Preheat oven to 375°. On work surface, form dough into one or two rolls 1 inch in diameter. Slice into sixty ½-inch rounds and arrange on baking sheets.
4. Slightly beat the remaining egg and brush over the rounds. Press 1 almond in the center of each round. Bake in preheated oven for 15 minutes until golden.

Sweets are not often a part of a Chinese dinner, but Americans like to eat dessert with Chinese food.

The Lexington

Dinner for Six

Chicken Liver Pâté

Scampi Adriatic

Wild Rice en Consommé

Pecan Pie

Wines:

With the Pâté—Louis M. Martini sherry

With the Scampi—Wente Pinot Chardonnay

Don Ryan, Manager

Jim Hennessey, Chef

THE LEXINGTON

Since 1935, the Lexington has been a fashionable place to congregate in St. Paul. State legislators informally caucus in the shadows of its Old English bar. Business cronies meet there once or twice a week, as they have done since their college days. Teenagers stop by in their finery on their way to the prom; their parents, who did the same, still frequently drop by for dinner. The Lex, as it is familiarly known, has always been a favorite choice for celebrations of all kinds: christening and wedding parties, engagement dinners, and "the sad times, too," recounts manager Don Ryan, "after a friend's funeral."

They find a rich history at the Lex. Barring his years of military service, Don has been there to greet clients since its doors opened. Many patrons were also sent overseas during World War II, but the Lex boys kept in touch. Their letters home were posted in the bar, and collected messages were relayed in return as a newsletter to their bases abroad. Furloughs found these regulars bellying up to the grand curving bar, where bartender Ed Knoepke never forgot a face or how an individual liked his cocktails.

Both veterans and non-veterans also find a rich tradition at the Lex. It is not only they and Don who can count many years of being there; many of the black-outfitted waitresses have worked there for twenty-five years. The splendid decor—characterized by French provincial paneling, gilt frames, plush burgundy colors, and beaded chandeliers—has been maintained rather than being updated to a more trendy style. And the American cuisine has never wavered in its excellence.

The tried-and-true menu is the product of John Donnelly, night chef for twenty-eight years, and day chef Jim Hennessey, a novice with only fourteen years in the kitchen. They have collaborated on a list that highlights prime rib—the perennial favorite—but also features outstanding scallopini, Minnesota pheasant, liver and onions, lamb shank, and braised short ribs. Each and every item served at the Lexington is made from scratch—from these entrées to the soups, breads, secret house salad dressing, and old-fashioned desserts. Like all of the other aspects of the restaurant, the cuisine rarely changes, because rarely can it be improved upon.

People may move away from St. Paul, but spiritually they are never far from the Lexington.

1096 Grand Avenue
St. Paul

THE LEXINGTON

CHICKEN LIVER PÂTÉ

1 cup butter
¾ cup minced onion
1 pound chicken livers
2 tablespoons sherry
2 tablespoons brandy
¾ cup Chicken Stock
  (see index)

⅛ teaspoon thyme
  Salt and pepper
1 package melba toast
  or crackers (optional)

1. In a sauté pan over medium heat, melt the butter; skim off foam and discard. Let stand until sediment has settled. Carefully pour the melted butter into a clean sauté pan, leaving behind the sediment. Discard the sediment and reheat the clarified butter over medium heat. Add the onion and sauté for 2 to 3 minutes. Add the chicken livers and sauté approximately 5 minutes until brown, stirring so all sides brown evenly.

2. Add the sherry, brandy, chicken stock, and thyme; cover pan and reduce heat. Simmer until most of the liquid has evaporated, approximately 15 minutes. Drain, reserving liquid.

3. Place the liver mixture in a blender or food processor and purée, adding salt and pepper to taste. If the mixture seems too stiff, add a little of the reserved liquid; if not, the liquid may be discarded. Chill in a bowl 6 to 8 hours.

4. At serving time, scoop mounds onto six small plates. Serve with melba toast or crackers, if desired.

THE LEXINGTON

SCAMPI ADRIATIC

1½ pounds butter
2 pounds shrimp, shelled
   and deveined
1 tablespoon minced garlic
1 onion, chopped
¼ cup canned chicken stock
   Dash of Worcestershire
   sauce (preferably Lea
   and Perrins)

2 tablespoons A-1 sauce
2 tablespoons prepared
   yellow mustard
½ cup Sauternes wine
⅓ cup tarragon vinegar
1 tablespoon oregano
2 tablespoons coarsely
   crushed tarragon leaves
   Salt and pepper

1. Preheat oven to 400°.
2. In a sauté pan over medium heat, melt ¼ pound plus 4 tablespoons of the butter; add the shrimp and sauté for 5 minutes, turning once. Place on an ovenproof serving platter and keep warm.
3. In a clean sauté pan over medium heat, melt 4 tablespoons of the butter; skim off foam and discard. Wipe out first sauté pan and carefully pour the melted butter into it, leaving sediment behind. Cut the remaining 1 pound butter into chunks. Set aside.
4. Over medium heat, sauté the garlic and onion in the clarified butter until soft, approximately 3 minutes. Add the chicken stock, Worcestershire sauce, A-1 sauce, mustard, wine, vinegar, oregano, and tarragon, and bring to a boil; immediately remove the sauce from the heat and with a whisk whip in the reserved chunks of butter.
5. Season to taste with salt and pepper. Pour sauce over platter of shrimp and bake 20 minutes. Serve hot.

This dish has been on our menu for years, and it remains one of the customers' favorites.

THE LEXINGTON

WILD RICE EN CONSOMMÉ

2 cups wild rice
½ cup butter
¼ cup finely chopped onion
¼ cup finely chopped celery
½ cup sliced mushrooms
1 tablespoon salt

2 cups canned beef bouillon
  or consommé
2 cups Chicken Stock
  (see index)
¼ cup sherry
½ cup chopped parsley

1. Place the rice in a sieve and wash under cold, running water; drain.
2. In a sauté pan over medium heat, melt the butter; add the onion, celery, mushrooms, rice, and salt; sauté approximately 5 minutes, stirring often.
3. Add the beef bouillon, chicken stock, and sherry. Cover the pan and lower heat. Simmer approximately 1 hour, or until tender.
4. To serve, spoon into a serving dish and fold in the chopped parsley.

On any given night here, you'll see a roomful of people you know, or at least have a nodding acquaintance with.

PECAN PIE

2 tablespoons butter
1 cup sugar
3 eggs
½ cup dark corn syrup
⅛ teaspoon salt
1 teaspoon vanilla extract

½ cup whipping cream
1½ cups coarsely
  chopped pecans
1 unbaked pie shell

1. Preheat oven to 400°.
2. In a mixing bowl, cream the butter; add the sugar gradually and continue to cream until the mixture is light and fluffy. Add the eggs, syrup, salt, vanilla, cream, and pecans and mix well.
3. Pour filling into the unbaked pie shell and bake in preheated oven for 35 minutes. When done, remove and cool slightly; then cut into six pieces and place on individual serving plates.

I've been making this for fourteen years here. It's simple and always popular; the hardest part is writing down the recipe!

Dinner for Six

Broccoli Soup

Swiss Pear Bread

Hearts of Palm Salad

Sweetbreads Lowell Inn, Mushroom Sauce

Old Fashioned Maple Frango

Wine:

Chateau Montelena Grgich Hills Cellars Zinfandel

Arthur and Maureen Palmer, Innkeepers, Owners, and Chefs

LOWELL INN

"V isitors who accidentally discover us act as if they've just caught a twenty-pound walleye," grins Arthur Palmer, Lowell Inn's proprietor. Most diners, however, make their travel to this restaurant a deliberate and much anticipated event, and never leave disappointed.

The "Mount Vernon of the West" has been luring guests for over fifty years to the small town of Stillwater on the bank of the St. Croix River. Its inaugural dinner on December 25, 1930, marked the day when Arthur's parents, Nelle and Arthur Palmer, unpacked their vaudevillian's suitcases for the last time and became innkeepers of the stately, white-pillared colonial mansion. Nelle decorated it in the Williamsburg style she had come to love during her travels, displaying her precious collection of Waterford crystal, Dresden china, and a wealth of antique Sheffield silver in the white-paneled George Washington dining room. Today the portraits of George and Martha continue to cast their approving smiles at the waitresses in their organdy aprons and gowns of flounced and embroidered batiste who maneuver service plates, adjust the crisp hand-crested Irish linen, and refill the goblets of jewel-bright pressed glass.

The patrons cannot see the care that goes into the preparation of their meals, but the presentation and flavors assure them that this work is done with devotion. Arthur takes advantage of the wares of hundreds of purveyors in his search for the perfect ingredient—a special lightly salted pork steak from a small Michigan farm, the best maple syrup from Vermont, Colorado mountain honey, Roquefort imported from France, chocolate from Holland, a Swiss blend of espresso, and so on. If what is available is not to his liking, he makes it himself: tarragon vinegar, raspberry brandy, or special cooking oils, to name a few. This extreme precision, however, does not make for a cuisine that is heavy or overdone. "We don't play games with our food. Our approach is to keep it simple but accentuate the flavor. It's basic, honest home cooking with no attempt to disguise the flavor."

To what does Arthur attribute the success of Lowell Inn? "Attention to detail: we've made that our first priority. And consistency. 'don't change a thing,' people tell me. 'You can't go out and buy memories like this.' "

102 North Second Street
Stillwater

LOWELL INN

BROCCOLI SOUP

2 tablespoons butter
2 tablespoons flour
2 cups milk
3 cups fresh broccoli
  florets with stems
1 medium-size onion,
  grated

1 teaspoon seasoned salt
¼ teaspoon pepper
½ cup whipping cream
  (optional)

1. Make a roux by blending the butter and the flour; in a large saucepan over medium heat, warm the milk. Stir in the roux, whisking until smooth to create a white sauce. Remove from heat.

2. Meanwhile, place the broccoli in another saucepan and add water to cover. Cook over medium heat until tender, approximately 5 minutes. Drain and discard liquid. Place the broccoli in an electric blender; blend until the broccoli is chopped medium-fine. Place in a bowl and add the onion, seasoned salt, and pepper; mix well. Stir the broccoli mixture into the white sauce and rewarm gently. If desired, add the cream a little at a time to thin. Serve hot.

Not tasting the food under the sauce may be the French way, but honoring its true flavor is our approach here. Ever since my father taught himself how to cook and he taught me, we've learned to keep it simple.

LOWELL INN

SWISS PEAR BREAD

½ cup diced prunes
½ cup diced dried pears
¼ cup raisins
¼ cup currants
¼ cup diced citron
¼ cup diced candied
   orange peel
¼ cup diced candied
   lemon peel
1 teaspoon cinnamon
1 teaspoon ground anise

1 teaspoon whole anise
1 teaspoon ground cloves
2 tablespoons dry yeast
2 tablespoons prune juice
2 tablespoons butter
⅓ cup sugar
½ teaspoon salt
1 tablespoon brandy
5 to 6 cups flour
   (approximately)

1. A day in advance, place the first eleven ingredients in a large sauce-pan. Add water to cover and cook over low heat for ½ hour. Drain the fruit and reserve the liquid.
2. Stir the yeast into the prune juice and let stand in a warm place (75°) for 5 to 7 minutes.
3. Meanwhile, place ¼ cup of the warm liquid reserved from the fruits in a large mixing bowl. Add the butter, stirring to melt. Add the yeast mixture, sugar, salt, brandy, and 2 cups of the flour. Beat well to mix. Continuing to beat hard, add the remaining flour 1 cup at a time, until the dough forms a ball and sides of the bowl are clean.
4. On a lightly floured surface, knead the dough until elastic, 7 to 10 minutes. Roll dough into a rectangle the length of a bread loaf pan. Roll up the width, jellyroll style, to form a loaf shape. Place the dough in a bread loaf pan and cover tightly with plastic wrap. Refrigerate overnight.
5. Remove pan from refrigerator, cover loosely with the plastic wrap, and allow dough to rise 2 hours in a warm place.
6. Preheat oven to 300°.
7. Bake in preheated oven 1 hour. Remove when done and place on a rack to cool. After 10 minutes of cooling, remove bread from pan and let cool further. To serve, slice in ¼-inch slices.

People's memories have a way of making things seem better. Maybe someone enjoyed our pear bread thirty years ago. It's very difficult to make it taste as wonderful as that person remembers. The pressure is on us to recreate the exact experience.

HEARTS OF PALM SALAD

1 head Bibb lettuce, coarsely torn	1 (8-ounce) can black olives, pits removed
1 (1-pound) can hearts of palm, drained	½ cup soy sauce
1 medium-size cucumber, peeled	½ teaspoon freshly ground pepper

1. Divide the lettuce on six individual serving plates. Top with the hearts of palm.
2. Slice or coarsely chop the cucumber and sprinkle over the hearts of palm. Slice the olives and sprinkle on top of salad.
3. Season the soy sauce with the pepper and drizzle over the salad. Serve immediately.

This salad is a little off the beaten path, and it has a nice little diet-oriented dressing, for a change of flavor and pace.

SWEETBREADS LOWELL INN, MUSHROOM SAUCE

6 (3-ounce) clusters veal sweetbreads	6 (½-inch) slices firm white bread
6 peppercorns	MUSHROOM SAUCE (see next page)
2 tablespoons lemon juice	
1 cup fine cracker crumbs	6 tablespoons toasted almonds
1 cup flour	
½ cup oil	3 tablespoons minced parsley
2 eggs	2 tablespoons paprika
1 cup milk	1 (8-ounce) bottle chutney

1. In a 6-quart saucepan, place the sweetbreads with the peppercorns and water to cover. Add the lemon juice and boil over medium-high heat 15 to 20 minutes, or until the sweetbreads turn white. Drain, reserving stock for the Mushroom Sauce. Let the sweetbreads cool until easy to handle, then clean out veins and membranes and discard.

(continued next page)

2. Combine the crumbs and the flour. Coat the sweetbreads in this mixture. Heat the oil in a skillet. Over medium heat, pan-fry the sweetbreads approximately 2 minutes on each side, turning once. Remove and keep warm.

3. Lightly beat the eggs with the milk. Dip the bread slices in this wash. Fry three of the bread slices in the skillet approximately 1 minute on each side. Repeat with the remaining three slices.

4. Arrange the fried bread on a serving platter and set the sweetbreads on top. Pour the Mushroom Sauce over; sprinkle with the toasted almonds, parsley, and paprika. Add spoonfuls of the chutney for garnish.

MUSHROOM SAUCE

1 quart stock (reserved from the Sweetbreads)	¼ teaspoon white pepper
1 stalk celery, chopped	1 teaspoon Ranch dressing (prepared)
½ large onion, chopped	1 cup whipping cream
Bouquet garni:	½ cup plus 2 tablespoons butter
1 sprig parsley	2 tablespoons flour
1 bay leaf	2 cups coarsely chopped mushrooms
1 sprig thyme	
1 sprig basil	
½ teaspoon salt	

1. In a large saucepan, bring the stock to a boil over high heat and boil 20 minutes. Add the celery, onion, bouquet garni, salt, pepper, Ranch dressing, and cream. Reduce heat and simmer over low heat 5 minutes.

2. Meanwhile, make a roux by blending the 2 tablespoons butter with the flour. Stir into the sauce, whisking to blend. Keep warm over low heat.

3. In a skillet, heat the remaining ½ cup butter and sauté the mushrooms over medium heat until just tender, approximately 2 minutes. Stir into the sauce and serve.

Every time I travel I taste something I like and start tracking it down. Intellectually, I disapprove of dealing with so many sources of supplies, but here we fall in love with all our vendors! It's the same with the Inn's antiques. We never stop buying beautiful things. Every time a box comes, it's like Christmas.

LOWELL INN

OLD FASHIONED MAPLE FRANGO

½ cup maple syrup
3 tablespoons honey
   or corn syrup

3 egg yolks, lightly beaten
2 cups whipping cream

1. In a small saucepan, warm the syrup and honey slightly. Add the egg yolks in a slow, steady stream. Gently boil over medium heat until the mixture thickens and coats a metal spoon, approximately 6 to 8 minutes. Remove from heat and allow to cool to room temperature, approximately ½ hour.
2. Whip the cream until firm peaks form; gently fold the cream into the maple mixture. Pour into a loaf pan and freeze several hours or overnight, or until firm.
3. To serve, dip the pan briefly into a larger pan of warm water and unmold onto a plate. Serve in ¾-inch slices on individual plates.

Eating is always a new delight for me, whether I'm camping out with a kettle of fish or sampling a soufflé.

Dinner for Six

Mussel Saffron Soup

Belgian Endive Salad with Hazelnut Oil Vinaigrette

Broiled Sirloin with Sauce Paloise

Floating Islands with Fresh Raspberry Sauce

Wines:

Jordan Sonoma Cabernet Sauvignon, 1977
or
Burgess Cellars Napa, 1978

Laurence Jeffery, Managing Director

Stephen Evans, General Manager

Paul O'Brien, Director of Food and Beverages

Andreas Sellner, Executive Chef

For ten years, a boudoir-like restaurant tucked into an alcove on the third level of the Marquette Inn catered to the aristocracy in Minneapolis. The Inn's discerning patrons dined there. Visiting film and opera stars and international artists and authors slipped incognito into recesses of soft salmon plush and beaded chandeliers, areas made very private by lace-veiled windows. The dining room also won a club-like following among the local cognoscenti, who weren't telling. The Marquis restaurant became the best-kept secret in town.

But secrets like that are too precious to husband, and now the word is out—as are a few of the venerable cobwebs. The formal French service that spoke to the seventies has been eliminated. Elegant simplicity has replaced ostentation, just as soft pastels and patterned china have replaced the original pristine whiteness of the tables. A creative new signature menu has retired the tableside tournedos and chateaubriands in vogue ten years ago.

The new wizard in the kitchen is Executive Chef Andreas Sellner, who brings with him much professional experience. A native Bavarian, he trained in Baden-Baden, went on to hotel posts in St. Moritz, Karlsruhe, and São Paolo, and then to dining rooms on America's east coast before arriving in Minnesota. "He brings the best standards in the business," attest his sous-chefs, who willingly deliver the inventive design, precision, and professional dedication he demands of them. "We will not compromise on consistency and quality," Andreas affirms, and the menu testifies to that. A meal at the Marquis might begin with turbot in a fresh tomato-basil vinaigrette with salmon quenelles or with artichokes with chicken mousse. Inspired soups follow: cold papaya soup, kirsch-laced quail consommé or the Mussel-Saffron Soup whose recipe is included here. Salads, such as Italian radicchio or Belgian endive swathed in hazelnut oil, next show off the chef's international flair. Veal medallions set over a sauce of watercress and chives is an entrée typical of the chef's inventiveness, which banishes flour-heavy sauces and large portions in favor of delicate reductions. To accompany the entrée, perhaps hand-sculpted carrots, a bright purée of beets, or a nut and chopped spinach custard.

Marquette Inn
710 Marquette Avenue
Minneapolis

MUSSEL SAFFRON SOUP

1½ quarts mussels,
  washed and debearded
2 cups good-quality
  dry white wine
4 shallots, minced
3 tablespoons butter
2 tablespoons olive oil
2 onions, coarsely chopped
2 leeks, cleaned and
  coarsely chopped
4 ripe tomatoes, blanched,
  peeled, seeded, and diced
  Bouquet garni:
  1 sprig parsley
  1 bay leaf
  1 sprig thyme
  1 teaspoon fennel seeds

4 cloves garlic, chopped
1 (6-ounce) firm-fleshed fish
  fillet (halibut, whiting,
  or turbot)
3 cups whipping cream
  Pinch of Spanish saffron
1 tablespoon sea salt
  Pinch of cayenne pepper
6 (1-inch) slices firm
  French bread
¼ cup freshly grated
  Parmesan cheese

1. In a stockpot, combine the mussels, wine, and half the shallots. Over medium heat, steam 6 to 8 minutes, or until the mussels open. Discard any that do not open. Remove the mussels from the shells and set aside. Discard the shells.
2. Strain the cooking liquid through a sieve lined with dampened cheesecloth and reserve.
3. In a Dutch oven, melt 2 tablespoons of the butter over low heat; add the olive oil. Slowly sweat the onions and leeks in the oil and butter until transparent, approximately 10 minutes; do not brown. Add the tomatoes, the reserved cooking liquid, bouquet garni, garlic, fish fillet, and 1 quart water. Simmer over low heat for 45 minutes.
4. Remove and purée in a food processor; strain. Return the strained mixture to the stockpot and add the cream. Stir in the saffron, salt, and cayenne pepper. Reheat over low heat while making croutons.

(continued next page)

5. In a skillet over medium heat, melt the remaining 1 tablespoon butter and sauté the bread 1 minute on each side until lightly browned.

6. To serve, ladle the soup into individual bowls. Float one crouton on each bowl and sprinkle with the Parmesan cheese.

Really good food can be expensive, but the customer is aware of quality and is willing to pay for it. We are able to get better seafood today than even a year ago.

BELGIAN ENDIVE SALAD WITH HAZELNUT OIL VINAIGRETTE

2 tablespoons red wine vinegar
2 tablespoons lemon juice
¼ teaspoon mustard
1½ cups olive oil
2 tablespoons hazelnut oil
¼ teaspoon salt

⅛ teaspoon freshly ground black pepper
2 heads Belgian endive, rinsed
2 heads Boston lettuce
2 large ripe tomatoes

1. In a small bowl, combine the vinegar, lemon juice, and mustard. Slowly add the olive oil and hazelnut oil, whisking constantly. Season with the salt and pepper.
2. Break the endive into individual leaves. Core, wash, and dry the Boston lettuce. Place the greens in a salad bowl; slice the tomatoes and add.
3. Just before serving, toss with the prepared dressing and serve on large, individual plates.

Heavy haute cuisine is on the way out. People are asking for more plain and simple food. We got rid of a lot of the excess baggage of fussy French service and ostentatious waiters. Today, the serving staff is excellent—I can't say enough about the importance of having good help. We encourage open communication between the kitchen and the front of the house.

BROILED SIRLOIN WITH SAUCE PALOISE

6 (6 to 8-ounce) prime
   sirloin filets, trimmed
   of all fat and silverskin
2 tablespoons chopped
   shallots
2 scant tablespoons
   freshly ground black
   pepper

3 tablespoons chopped
   fresh mint
¾ cup red wine vinegar
3 egg yolks
¾ pound unsalted
   butter, melted
1 teaspoon salt
   (approximately)

1. Broil the sirloin filets approximately 3 minutes per side, or until medium rare. Keep warm.
2. To make Sauce Paloise, place the shallots, pepper, 2 tablespoons of the mint, and vinegar in a saucepan. Cook over medium heat until all liquid is evaporated, approximately 5 minutes.
3. Put this reduction, the egg yolks, and 1 tablespoon water into a 2-quart mixing bowl that can withstand direct heat. Whisk this mixture over low heat approximately 2 minutes, or until it thickens and coats a spoon. Slowly whisk in the melted butter until a thick, creamy emulsion forms. Add the remaining 1 tablespoon mint and the salt to taste.
4. To serve, place the filets on individual heated plates and pour sauce on top of each.

FLOATING ISLANDS WITH FRESH RASPBERRY SAUCE

1½ cups egg whites
  (approximately 10 to 12)
1½ cups superfine sugar
2½ pints fresh ripe
  raspberries

¼ cup framboise liqueur
6 fresh mint leaves

1. In a large bowl of an electric mixer, beat the egg whites until soft peaks form. Begin adding the sugar in a steady stream and continue to beat for 5 to 10 minutes until it becomes a thick meringue.
2. In a large pot, heat approximately 2 quarts of water to simmering. Meanwhile, pour ice-cold water into another large pan.
3. With an ejector-style ice-cream scoop, place scoops of the meringue into the simmering water; do not allow water to boil. Poach 6 minutes on each side, turning once. Remove the meringues and place in the ice water for 5 minutes. Remove with slotted spoon and drain; store in a cool place until you are ready to serve.
4. Purée the raspberries in a blender with the liqueur. Strain through a fine sieve or chinois to remove the seeds.
5. To serve, pour some of the raspberry sauce into each of six large plates. Float several meringues on top of the sauce. Garnish each plate with a mint leaf.

We make our own baked goods and croissants and a few special desserts such as this one. The dessert list is small; we'd rather do three or four things and do them well.

MUFFULETTA

Dinner for Six

Fresh Broccoli Mousse with Mushroom Sauce

Spinach Salad with Vinaigrette Muffuletta

Fresh Scallops in Vouvray and Cream

Pears Poached in Wine

Wine:

Chateau Ste Michelle Johannisberg Riesling

Philip Roberts and Peter Mihajlov, Owners

Bill Demmer, Manager

Rick Boschee, Chef

MUFFULETTA

As a decorator, Phil Roberts often had the opportunity to design restaurants, but as he says, "Somewhere I crossed over the path, and the restaurant business fascinated me more than design." Longtime friend Peter Mihajlov's experience was largely limited to visiting many of the nation's top restaurants in the course of business travels. "We knew nothing about the business except that we liked to eat in nice places," the two partners now admit. However, when in 1976 an ideal location fell their way, they looked each other in the eye: "It's now or never." Thus was Muffuletta restaurant born.

They transformed a plywood-and-formica truck stop into a dining room of uptown chic. Its simple design scheme plays butcher block and breuer chairs in tones of toast against daisy-bright touches of white and yellow, softened by candles and flowers, hanging plants, and gentle currents of classical music. High shelves hold jars of pasta, cartons of Perrier, and tins of pomidoro—"a working storeroom that has a certain honesty."

Honesty and genuine pride in food preparation and its artful display are the hallmarks here. "We use nothing but the freshest foods," attests manager Bill Demmer. "We send back whole crates of strawberries if only one berry is bad. We want our procurers to realize that we won't settle for less than the very best." These standards of excellence also extend to Muffuletta's staff. "I shudder to think of the amount of training dollars spent, but we get it all back: our staff is so proud of where they work. We think of them as people first, employees second, telling them, "You are the vital link—the reputation of the restaurant lies with you.'"

The cuisine at Muffuletta knows no narrow ethnic bounds. It deliberately skirts such labels as French, Italian, or New Orleans—although its name is derived from that city's famous sandwich—so that its menu features a diverse variety of specialties. The restaurant's wine list is equally eclectic. "It's the emergence of a great new cuisine—the American Renaissance," explains Peter. "And Muffuletta is committed to being a leader in this emergence," Phil pledges. "Call it 'nouvelle American.' Our philosophy of 'special dishes from special places' gives us a gigantic playground."

2260 Como Avenue
St. Paul

FRESH BROCCOLI MOUSSE WITH MUSHROOM SAUCE

Butter
1 *pound broccoli florets*
  with ½" stems
1½ *cups whipping cream*
  Dash of nutmeg

Cracked black pepper
Juice of ½ lemon
4 *eggs*
  MUSHROOM SAUCE
  (see next page)

1. Preheat oven to 425°. Butter six individual molds.
2. Bring salted water to a boil in a saucepan. Blanch the broccoli in the boiling water for 4 to 5 minutes. Remove immediately and cool in ice water to retain bright green color. Drain well.
3. Bring the cream to boil in a skillet. Add the nutmeg, several grinds of pepper, lemon juice, and broccoli. Reduce heat and cook for 10 minutes.
4. Purée the broccoli/cream mixture together in an electric blender. Add the eggs one at a time, blending well after each addition.
5. Pour the mousse mixture into the molds until three-fourths full. Cover each mold with buttered foil. Place the molds in a pan and fill with boiling water to one-third their height. Bake in preheated oven for 25 to 30 minutes. Remove, cool slightly, and unmold. Serve each mousse on a bed of Mushroom Sauce.

Note: The mousse may be prepared 10 to 12 hours in advance and stored n the refrigerator. Reheat by baking in a water bath in a preheated 425° oven for 4 to 5 minutes.

MUFFULETTA

MUSHROOM SAUCE

1 teaspoon butter	Salt
2 tablespoons finely chopped shallots	Cracked black pepper
	¼ cup white wine
¼ pound mushrooms, quartered and sliced	½ cup whipping cream
	Dash of nutmeg

1. Heat the butter in a skillet and sauté the shallots for 2 to 3 minutes Add the mushrooms and sauté 2 to 3 minutes longer. Season with salt and pepper.
2. Deglaze the skillet with the white wine, simmering about 1 minute. Add the cream and bring to a boil. Lower heat and reduce 2 to 3 minutes until the sauce begins to thicken. Add the nutmeg and simmer 15 to 20 minutes longer. Keep warm until ready to serve.

We believe these dishes are excellent examples of what is surfacing as "American nouvelle." Readily available fresh foods are brought together and presented in a style that is pleasing both to the eye and the palate—yet, most important, these dishes are simple to prepare.

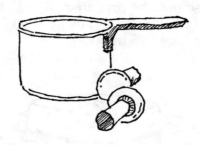

SPINACH SALAD WITH VINAIGRETTE MUFFULETTA

1 to 2 bunches fresh spinach,
    rinsed well and torn
½ cup sliced fresh mushrooms
¼ cup sliced water chestnuts
1 cup VINAIGRETTE
    MUFFULETTA

¼ cup crumbled bacon
¼ cup shredded Swiss cheese
1 hard-cooked egg, grated

In a salad bowl, combine the spinach, mushrooms, and water chestnuts. Toss with the Vinaigrette Muffuletta. Place the salad in chilled glass bowls. Top with the bacon, cheese, and egg. Serve at once.

VINAIGRETTE MUFFULETTA

1¾ cups salad oil
¼ cup white vinegar
¾ teaspoon dry mustard
½ clove garlic, finely
    chopped

2 tablespoons finely
    chopped onion
1 teaspoon salt
1½ teaspoons fresh cracked
    black pepper

At least one day in advance, combine all ingredients in a glass bowl or jar. Refrigerate, then stir or shake well before using.

Our focus is on foods indigenous to our local marketplaces and a style of preparation that reinforces current American tastes and lifestyles.

MUFFULETTA

FRESH SCALLOPS IN VOUVRAY AND CREAM

½ stalk celery	1¼ cups whipping cream
½ leek	2¼ pounds fresh sea scallops
1 carrot	6 tablespoons butter
1 cup Vouvray wine	

1. Cut the celery, leek, and carrot into thin 3-inch julienne strips. Set aside. Bring the Vouvray and the cream to a slow boil in a steamer or pot large enough to accommodate a basket for steaming.
2. Steam the scallops and vegetables in the basket over the Vouvray/cream mixture for 7 to 8 minutes. Be careful not to overcook; the scallops should just begin to turn firm and the vegetables should be crisp-tender.
3. Remove the scallops and vegetables. Make a bed of the vegetables on heated plates; arrange the scallops over. Reduce the Vouvray/cream mixture over moderate heat for 5 to 8 minutes, or until it begins to thicken. Remove from heat and add the butter. Swirl together and pour over scallops and vegetables. Serve immediately.

Be certain to remove the sauce from the heat before swirling in the butter. If it is too hot, the butter will separate.

A nice California chablis will also work well in this sauce. The wine served with the scallops, Chateau Ste. Michelle Johannisberg Riesling from Washington State, is an excellent example of a fine wine produced by a small winery outside of the more traditional growing areas.

PEARS POACHED IN WINE

6 *small pears*
2 *cups dry red wine*
1 *cup sugar*

2 *tablespoons lemon juice*
1 *stick cinnamon*

1. A day in advance, peel and core the pears from the bottom with an apple corer. Set aside.
2. Combine the wine, sugar, lemon juice, and cinnamon stick in a saucepan. Bring to a boil, stirring until the sugar has dissolved. Add the pears and partially cover the pan. Simmer on low heat for 15 to 20 minutes. The pears should be soft but not mushy.
3. Remove from heat to cool, then remove the pears carefully with a large spoon and place in a bowl. Pour the marinade over the pears and refrigerate overnight. Serve in individual dessert dishes with several spoonfuls of the chilled marinade.

As a variation, the dessert can be prepared with a dry white wine—a dry vermouth will work quite well.

Murray's

Dinner for Six

Hickory Smoked Shrimp

Green Salad with Roquefort Dressing

Broiled Filet Mignon

Murray's Strawberry Pie

Wine:

Jordan Sonoma Cabernet Sauvignon

Marie and Patrick J. Murray, Owners

Danny Brunette, Chef

In 1946, the family-owned Murray's restaurant was known as a very special supper club. "I don't think that has changed," says Pat Murray, who with his mother Marie upholds the Murray tradition set by his late father Arthur. "There's no change of philosophy from my Dad to myself. We've always cared for our customers. It's more than being a host—we believe in treating people like family. They mean a lot to us." Considering the popularity of Murray's, the restaurant must also mean a lot to the customers.

To enter Murray's is to step into a nightclub of the fifties. Under a movie-set, free-form ceiling, old gold valances drape mirrored walls and banquettes near a tiny dance floor. Garlanded sconces and wrought-iron grilles add an ornate New Orleans touch to the pink-clad tables and menus in matching pink that herald the award-winning butter-knife beef.

"My father made it his trademark," Pat says, "and it's still the best seller." It is no ordinary meat. The beef from Colorado steers is aged ninety days, then cut to specification in Murray's kitchen "so we're able to see it. If it doesn't look right, we send it back." The famous Murray marinade and seasonings which flavor it are a closely-guarded secret, but service of the meal for two on a sizzling platter is a proud and public presentation. The prime, char-broiled-to-perfection steak is sliced into ruddy pink ripples and presented with traditional steakhouse stand-bys of fluffy baked potatoes and a salad bowl topped with one of Marie's family-recipe dressings. Waitresses in pink-edged black deliver Murray's breadbasket, a homemade assortment of rye, garlic, melba, and salted pretzel twists. They return to tempt diners with dessert offerings such as an icebox pie that has pleased customers for twenty-five years and an excellent ice cream parfait.

To please the evolving tastes of the eighties, a few lighter touches have been added to the menu—a popular seafood catch of the day, several salad presentations, and Pat's pride, "an excellent veal T-bone steak broiled with fresh mushrooms. You don't see that anywhere." And seldom do you see a duplication of Pat Murray's credo: "The fact is, we give the finest beef and the finest service at the best possible price."

26 South Sixth Street
Minneapolis

HICKORY SMOKED SHRIMP

1½ pounds medium-size
    shrimp, shelled and
    deveined
2 cups French dressing
1 pound bacon
    (approximately)

1 (8-ounce) bottle cocktail
    sauce
1 lemon, cut in 6 wedges

1. Preheat broiler.
2. Dip the shrimp one at a time into the French dressing. Cut strips of the bacon in half to equal the number of shrimp. Wrap each shrimp with a half-strip of bacon. Place on a cookie sheet with a rim. Pour remaining French dressing over the shrimp.
3. Place under broiler for 5 minutes, or until the bacon is nearly cooked.
4. Serve immediately on individual plates, passing the cocktail sauce and lemon wedges.

This is really an excellent dish, our most-asked-for appetizer since the day we opened.

GREEN SALAD WITH ROQUEFORT DRESSING

1 *large head iceberg*
    lettuce, coarsely torn
2 *tomatoes, each*
    cut in 6 wedges

12 *black olives,*
     pits removed
ROQUEFORT DRESSING

In individual salad bowls, divide the lettuce and top with the tomatoes, olives, and Roquefort Dressing. Serve immediately.

MURRAY'S

ROQUEFORT DRESSING

¼ pound Roquefort cheese
1 (8-ounce) carton
  sour cream
2 to 3 teaspoons sugar
¼ teaspoon seasoning salt
⅛ teaspoon garlic powder

1 tablespoon lemon juice
1 tablespoon apple cider
  vinegar
1 tablespoon salad oil
¾ cup whipping cream
½ teaspoon chopped chives

1. In a small mixing bowl, combine all ingredients and whisk until blended.
2. Mix at low speed with electric beaters for 2 to 3 minutes, or until the cheese and sour cream become well blended.

Note: Store any unused dressing in the refrigerator.

This has been our most popular dressing over the years, the family's recipe. We do everything from scratch—it's our belief. It costs us a lot more, but we think the extra ingredients are worth it. It's the best way to operate.

BROILED FILET MIGNON

4 teaspoons garlic salt or
   Lawry's seasoning salt
6 (½-pound) center cuts
   beef tenderloin

6 strips bacon
6 (¼"-thick) slices onion
6 large mushroom caps
½ bunch parsley

1. Preheat broiler. Rub the garlic or seasoning salt evenly over the filets.
2. Broil 4 minutes on one side. Remove and wrap one strip of bacon around the circumference of each filet. Secure with a toothpick. Turn the filets. Place one of the onion slices and one of the mushroom caps on each and broil another 4 minutes, or until medium rare.
3. When broiled, transfer to heated dinner plates, garnish with the parsley and serve immediately.

Steak has always been the specialty of the house; we've done a good job with steak throughout the years. We buy the best and use our special seasoning— a family secret. We recommend you substitute garlic salt, Lawry's seasoning salt, or just salt and pepper. Whichever seasoning you prefer, be sure to season the meat before broiling, so the flavor is cooked in deeply. If you season the meat after broiling instead of before, you just taste the salt.

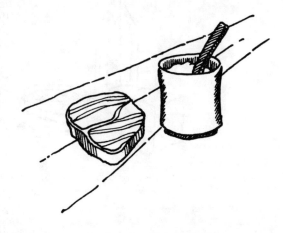

MURRAY'S STRAWBERRY PIE

1½ tablespoons cornstarch
2 cups sugar
  Pinch of salt
  Dash of red food coloring
1 quart strawberries,
  washed and hulled
1 (9") baked pie crust

1 cup whipping cream,
  chilled
2 tablespoons confectioners'
  sugar
1 teaspoon vanilla extract

1. Dissolve the cornstarch in ½ cup cold water. In a small saucepan, bring 2 cups water to boil. Add the dissolved cornstarch and boil 2 minutes. Add the sugar, stirring to dissolve. Boil 3 to 4 minutes. Add the salt and a few drops of food coloring.

2. Allow filling to cool slightly, approximately 1 hour. Mix in the strawberries, then pour into the baked pie crust. Chill well.

3. With chilled bowl and beaters, whip the cream until stiff, while gradually incorporating the confectioners' sugar and vanilla extract. Slice the pie and top each serving with a dollop of the whipped cream.

In this restaurant, my mother and I don't say, "this is mine, this is yours, this is ours"—there's a sharing between us. This recipe has been a favorite of both of ours for twenty-five years.

Dinner for Six

Moules à la Marinière

Gigot d'Agneau Rôti aux Aromates

Mixed Green Salad

Reine de Saba

Espresso

Beverages:

Before dinner—Vermouth Cassis

With the Moules—Freemark Abbey Napa Chardonnay, 1979

*With the Gigot d'Agneau—Château Cos d'Estournel,
Haut-Médoc, 1978*

After the Espresso—Martell Cognac Cordon Bleu

Lynne Alpert, Proprietor

THE NEW FRENCH CAFE

The New French Cafe was opened in 1977 by two women with no formal training in cooking, no management experience, and no background in marketing. The part of town was wrong, the staff all new and untrained, and the cuisine a far cry from the steakhouse staples of the day. But despite the odds, the New French Cafe became an instant success. "We felt our idea was strong enough that people would come to us. We knew we'd be successful—but we had no idea how quickly!" admits Lynne Alpert, now sole owner.

"Today food is more direct and straightforward," she declares, which enables her to serve food which has what she calls a "rustic edge": "I don't like a purée. I like to really taste the ingredients with no artifice." In keeping with that mandate, freshness and quality define the cuisine at the New French Cafe—insistence on imported oils and vinegars, specially selected chocolate, and a fine wine list that the self-taught proprietor has assembled. But Lynne considers factors other than these as well. "Nouvelle cuisine presumes a lot of money, both on the part of people eating and cooking. It uses only the choicest parts of everything. Now we are paying attention to the rest, and our menus reflect these changes. When we cut a veal chop off the loin, we'll use the trimmings for a stock or terrine."

Lynne has assembled a talented and loyal kitchen staff to whom she gives the reins to devise the menus that change with the seasons. Here there is no splintering of assignments into prep cook, sauté chef, or saucier. Each cook is a complete craftsman who takes resonsibility for each order from start to well-sauced finish. "That's part of the pleasure of cooking," Lynne states. "I give them the opportunity to choose to make something themselves: 'This is the fish of the day; how shall we use it?' We don't do the same thing twice. One nice thing that happens at this cafe: the menu and the food change with the experience of the people who work here."

The decor is deliberately simple: bare walls and overhead ducts given a slick of white paint; baskets and tubs of fresh blooms in the storefront windows; an open-to-view kitchen and roaring espresso machine that adds to the hum of activity which starts with an early morning's steaming croissant and continues through a candlelit dinner hour.

128 North Fourth Street
Minneapolis

THE NEW FRENCH CAFE

MOULES A LA MARINIÈRE

6 quarts mussels	¼ teaspoon thyme
¼ cup minced green onions	6 tablespoons butter
¼ cup minced shallots	2 cups light dry white wine
½ cup chopped parsley	French bread (optional)
½ bay leaf	

1. If using uncultured mussels, scrub thoroughly under cold running water. Cut off the beards and scrape off barnacles. Soak mussels in cold water at least 2 hours, discarding any that float. Drain.
2. In a deep saucepan with a tight-fitting lid, place the green onions, shallots, ¼ cup of the chopped parsley, bay leaf, thyme, butter, and wine. Bring to a boil over high heat and cook 2 to 3 minutes.
3. Add the mussels, cover, and steam 5 minutes, occasionally shaking and jerking the pot to ensure even cooking. Do not lift lid.
4. When the mussels have opened, remove pan from heat. Lift the mussels from the hot stock with a large strainer or slotted spoon. Discard any that have not opened. Place the shells containing the mussels in six large soup bowls. Strain the stock, then ladle it into each bowl and sprinkle with the remaining ¼ cup chopped parsley. Serve at once with crusty French bread.

Cultured mussels are frequently available; they come in absolutely clean. You just go ahead and cook them.

Today the public is more interested in food than it was a few years ago, studying on its own, thinking in new ways about it. There's more sophistication.

GIGOT D'AGNEAU RÔTI AUX AROMATES

1 (5 to 6-pound) leg of lamb,
  with most fat removed
3 garlic cloves, peeled
⅓ teaspoon thyme
⅓ teaspoon savory
⅓ teaspoon oregano
⅓ teaspoon marjoram

½ cup olive oil
  Salt and pepper
⅓ cup white wine
1 tablespoon butter, diced
  GREEN BEANS
  GRILLED TOMATO

1. Preheat oven to 425°.
2. Rub the entire leg of lamb with the garlic cloves. Combine the thyme, savory, oregano, and marjoram. Sprinkle the herbs over the lamb to cover, then rub on the olive oil to ensure even distribution. Just before roasting, sprinkle with salt and pepper.
3. Place the roast in a heavy shallow pan and roast in preheated oven about 1 hour. After first 10 minutes, reduce heat to 325° and continue roasting until done, basting the last 10 minutes with the accumulated pan juices.
4. Remove roast from oven and let rest in warm spot for 10 minutes to allow meat to relax. Place on a carving platter and set aside.
5. Skim fat from roasting pan; place pan over high heat. Pour in the wine and reduce by two-thirds while stirring and scraping with a wooden spoon to dislodge and dissolve the drippings.
6. Remove from heat and swirl in the butter to create a light-bodied, velvety sauce. Carve the meat and place on heated dinner plates; serve the sauce separately. Garnish the plates with the Green Beans and Grilled Tomato.

Note: The roasting time should be 10 minutes per pound.

This recipe is good because you can use the same treatment on lamb noisettes or chops; the butcher will cut these for you.

The feeling about food has changed in the past five years. Today more people are not only using the choicest parts of everything, in the nouvelle style, but paying attention to the rest of the duck or artichoke or whatever it is. You can't throw that away. Maybe it will show up in a soup or terrine.

GREEN BEANS

1 *pound fresh green beans*   1 *teaspoon salt*
1 *tablespoon butter,*
   at room temperature

1. Snap off the ends and remove the strings from the green beans. Rinse under cold water and drain.
2. Place the beans in a saucepan and add water to cover. Bring to a boil and blanch 7 minutes; drain immediately.
3. Return beans to saucepan; do not add water. Heat ½ minute to dry. Add the butter and salt and toss to coat evenly. Serve at once.

GRILLED TOMATO

3 *large firm tomatoes*   2 *teaspoons good-quality*
   olive oil

1. Preheat broiler.
2. Slice the tomatoes in half through the middle. Sprinkle the cut surfaces with the olive oil. Broil 3 to 5 minutes, or until lightly browned. Serve at once.

MIXED GREEN SALAD

2 *cups torn romaine lettuce*	¾ *cup good-quality Italian*
2 *cups torn Bibb lettuce*	*or French olive oil*
2 *cups curly endive*	¼ *cup French wine vinegar*

1. Rinse the salad greens and pat dry. Chill to crisp. When crisp, place in a salad bowl.
2. Combine the olive oil and vinegar in a jar with a screw-top lid. Shake well and pour over the greens. Toss lightly to coat evenly. Serve at once.

Note: Do not add or substitute with iceberg lettuce.

REINE DE SABA

¼ *pound semisweet chocolate*	3 *eggs, separated*
2 *tablespoons brewed*	⅓ *cup pulverized almonds*
espresso coffee	¼ *teaspoon almond extract*
¼ *pound butter, at room*	¾ *cup cake flour*
temperature	*CHOCOLATE BUTTER*
⅔ *cup plus 1 tablespoon*	*GLAZE*
sugar	

1. Preheat oven to 350°. Butter and flour an 8-inch cake pan.
2. In a double boiler placed over simmering water, melt the chocolate with the coffee. Remove from heat and cool.
3. In a small mixing bowl, cream the butter with the ⅔ cup sugar until pale yellow and fluffy. Add the egg yolks and beat until well blended.
4. Beat the egg whites in a separate bowl until soft peaks are formed. Sprinkle on the remaining 1 tablespoon sugar and beat until stiff peaks are formed.
5. Blend the cooled chocolate into the butter/egg mixture. Stir in the pulverized almonds and the almond extract. Immediately stir in part of the beaten egg whites to lighten the batter.

6. Fold the remaining egg whites and the cake flour alternately into the batter until completely incorporated. Turn into the cake pan and bake in preheated oven for 25 minutes. Remove and cool in pan for 10 minutes and reverse onto a rack. Cool completely, then frost with the Chocolate Butter Glaze.

Today people understand this restaurant. I don't have complaints about small portions, underdone food, or serving temperature any longer. People trust me: that's satisfying.

CHOCOLATE BUTTER GLAZE

3 ounces semisweet
    chocolate

6 tablespoons unsalted butter,
    at room temperature

Gradually melt the chocolate over low heat; remove from heat and let cool completely. When cool, mix in the butter 1 tablespoon at a time with a wooden spoon. Spread evenly over the cooled cake.

ORION ROOM

Dinner for Six

Curried Crab-Filled Mushrooms

Minnesota Wild Rice Soup

Poached Salmon with Sauce Beurre Blanc

Orion Salad with House Dressing

Strawberries Devonshire

Wines:

William Hill Napa Chardonnay, 1979
or
Shafer Napa Chardonnay, 1980

Brian O'Day, Manager
Jack Shapansky, Chef

At the summit of Minneapolis's tallest building, the Orion Room is poised fifty stories above the heartbeat of the city, close to the constellation from which it draws its name. The elevator ride up transports one to an extraordinary world where the city itself makes up much of the decor. Vast walls of glass display the panorama of trees, lakes, and local landmarks far below. At night the highway lights traversing the town compete with the brightness of stars. Inside, the furnishings are dominated by a modern brass sculpture of Orion the Hunter on the room's farthest wall. It is sleek and chic, a chrome and chocolate-colored dining room in which green plants carve out private alcoves.

The Orion Room opened as a private club in 1972, but several years ago its management decided that the dining public deserved a restaurant "fifty stories above the ordinary." Discarding its former French style, it has become proudly American with a new lighter menu that highlights seafood flown in fresh four times a week and the choice beef that made the Midwest famous. There are the foods that are Minnesota's forte: walleyed pike in pine nuts and pistachios and wild rice soup that marries the precious grain with rich broth, heavy cream, and savory seasonings.

"We try to be all-American and darn good at what we do," declares the staff. "Fresh products aren't more expensive; they just take more care." Giving that constant care is young chef Jack Shapansky, a culinary Institute graduate and son of a local pastry chef, who supervises the kitchen, and manager Brian O'Day, who learned the skills of fine service at Cornell University's hotel management program. "A year ago," they say, "we made a statement with our wines. We've become an American restaurant and are very pro-California wines. With ninety labels, ours is the most extensive California list in the city." They present the cellar list in the same way they present all of the factors of the Orion Room—with pride.

50th Floor, IDS Tower
Nicollet Mall
Minneapolis

ORION ROOM

CURRIED CRAB-FILLED MUSHROOMS

¾ pound flaked crabmeat
¾ cup CURRY SAUCE
2 dozen large mushrooms,
 cleaned and stems
 removed

1½ cups GLAÇAGE
 (see next page)

1. Preheat oven to 350°.
2. Combine the crabmeat and the Curry Sauce and stuff into the mushrooms. Place the stuffed mushrooms on a cookie sheet and bake in preheated oven approximately 10 to 15 minutes. Remove from oven and preheat broiler.
3. Top the mushrooms with the Glaçage and brown slightly under the broiler, approximately 1 to 2 minutes. Remove and place four mushrooms each on six individual serving plates; serve while hot.

CURRY SAUCE

1 medium-size apple,
 chopped
1 small onion, chopped
1 medium-size banana,
 chopped
¾ cup apple juice
½ can Coco Lopez

½ cup Major Grey's chutney
2 cups Chicken Stock
 (see index)
½ cup shredded coconut
¼ cup butter
⅓ cup flour
3 tablespoons curry powder

1. In a saucepan over medium heat, combine the apple, onion, banana, apple juice, Coco Lopez, chutney, chicken stock, and coconut. Bring to a boil.
2. Meanwhile, make a roux by mixing the butter and the flour. Blend in the curry powder. Add to the boiling stock, beating to mix thoroughly. Reduce heat and simmer for 1 hour to obtain at least 1¼ cups of sauce. Let cool.

The Coco Lopez juice is a canned coconut milk available in gourmet groceries and liquor stores.

ORION ROOM

GLAÇAGE

¼ cup whipping cream,
 chilled

½ cup HOLLANDAISE
 SAUCE, at room
 temperature

½ cup CURRY SAUCE,
 at room temperature

With chilled bowl and beaters, whip the cream until stiff. Combine ½ cup of the whipped cream with the Hollandaise Sauce and the Curry Sauce.

HOLLANDAISE SAUCE

6 tablespoons butter
1 egg yolk
⅛ teaspoon salt
   Pinch of pepper

3 dashes of Tabasco sauce
   Dash of Worcestershire
   sauce
Juice of ½ lemon

1. Clarify the butter by melting it in a sauté pan over medium heat and skimming off and discarding any foam.
2. In the top pan of a double boiler placed over simmering water, combine the egg yolk, 1 tablespoon water, salt, pepper, and Tabasco and Worcestershire sauces. While continuously whipping the mixture, add the clarified butter in a slow, steady stream, leaving behind the sediment. Whisk 3 to 5 minutes until all butter is incorporated, then remove from heat.
3. Whisking briefly, add the lemon juice. Let cool.

This is the appetizer that gets the most compliments in the kitchen. The Curry Sauce with its elusive blend of fruit and chutney flavors sets off the crab and mushroom combination to perfection.

MINNESOTA WILD RICE SOUP

¼ cup butter
¼ cup raw wild rice
2 tablespoons blanched
   sliced almonds
½ cup finely diced onion

½ cup finely diced celery
½ cup finely diced carrot
   SOUP STOCK
2 teaspoons arrowroot (optional)
2 cups whipping cream

In a heavy pan, melt the butter over medium heat and sauté the wild rice, almonds, onion, celery, and carrot for 2 to 3 minutes. Add the Soup Stock and simmer over low heat for 1¼ hours, skimming occasionally to remove scum. If necessary, thicken with the arrowroot dissolved in ¼ cup of cream. Stir in the remaining cream just before serving. Serve in individual serving bowls.

SOUP STOCK

   Carcasses from 2 ducks
     or chickens
1 smoked ham bone
1 medium-size onion,
   sliced
1 tablespoon Maggi
   seasoning or Knorr-Swiss
   Aromat seasoning

   Salt and white pepper
     to taste
1 bay leaf
¼ stalk celery, chopped
2 carrots, chopped

In a large kettle over medium heat, combine the carcasses, ham bone, onion, Maggi seasoning, salt and pepper, bay leaf, celery, carrots and 1¼ quarts water. Bring to a boil; reduce heat to low and simmer approximately 1½ hours. Strain.

Since we opened in 1972, this recipe honoring Minnesota wild rice has remained one of the most popular items on our menu. People from out of state return especially to taste this soup again.

ORION ROOM

POACHED SALMON WITH SAUCE BEURRE BLANC

1 carrot
1 stalk celery
1 shallot
1 bay leaf
½ teaspoon chopped fresh
  thyme

6 (6-ounce) fillets of
  fresh salmon
SAUCE BEURRE BLANC

1. Coarsely chop the carrot, celery, and shallot; place them in a large stockpot. Add the bay leaf and thyme and approximately 2 cups water, or enough to cover the fish. Bring to a boil over medium heat; reduce heat to a simmer and place the fillets in the simmering water. Cook until just tender, approximately 6 to 8 minutes.
2. With a slotted spoon, remove the fillets and arrange on a warmed serving platter. Cover with Sauce Beurre Blanc.

SAUCE BEURRE BLANC

1 quart whipping cream
4 tablespoons butter,
  at room temperature

2 cups Chardonnay wine
2 shallots, finely chopped

1. Place the cream and the butter in a heavy saucepan; bring to a boil over medium heat. Immediately reduce heat and simmer until reduced by half, approximately 15 minutes.
2. Meanwhile, pour the wine into another saucepan; add the shallots and reduce over medium heat to ¼ cup, approximately 15 minutes.
3. Add the reduced cream to the reduced wine. Simmer 1 to 2 minutes to blend flavors. Strain to remove shallots.

I'm very pleased with our new menu because it's lighter. We're proud of the quality of our fish that it features. The seafood we feature is wholesome, it's consistent in quality, and it has become very popular with our dining public.

ORION SALAD WITH HOUSE DRESSING

1 *large head romaine lettuce, washed*
1 *(12-ounce) package croutons*
1 *(6-ounce) can garbanzo beans, drained*

6 *tablespoons freshly grated Parmesan cheese*
HOUSE DRESSING

1. Coarsely chop the romaine and place in a large salad bowl. Add the croutons, garbanzo beans, and Parmesan cheese.
2. Just before serving, toss with the House Dressing to taste. Serve on individual plates.

HOUSE DRESSING

½ *teaspoon sugar*
1 *cup Miracle Whip salad dressing*
1 *teaspoon Maggi seasoning*
4 *teaspoons lemon juice*
5 *teaspoons red wine vinegar*

1 *scant teaspoon finely chopped parsley*
2¼ *teaspoons finely chopped onion*
⅛ *teaspoon black pepper*
Pinch of garlic powder

1. In an electric blender, combine the sugar, Miracle Whip, Maggi seasoning, lemon juice, vinegar, parsley, onion, pepper, and garlic powder. Blend at low speed for 2 to 3 minutes.
2. Cover and refrigerate for 24 hours to blend flavors.

We've decided to de-formalize, to take the waiters out of their tuxedos. The Orion Room has become more relaxed. But we haven't changed the House Dressing: we get constant requests for its recipe.

ORION ROOM

STRAWBERRIES DEVONSHIRE

½ cup sour cream
1½ cups whipping cream,
   whipped until stiff
1 tablespoon brown sugar
1 tablespoon Grand Marnier

1 tablespoon Curaçao
Juice of ¼ orange
Juice of 1/6 lemon
1 quart fresh strawberries,
   rinsed and hulled

1. Combine the sour cream, ¾ cup of the whipped cream, the brown sugar, Grand Marnier, Curaçao, and orange and lemon juice; combine thoroughly.
2. Place the strawberries in six compote glasses. Pour a little of the sauce over. Top with additional whipped cream, if desired, and pass the remaining sauce in a sauceboat.

We prepare this dessert to order. It highlights our preference for fresh, light, wholesome foods given an extra-special touch.

PRONTO
RISTORANTE ™

Dinner for Six

Antipasto di Mare Rivierasco

Pasta Primavera

Petto di Pollo al Amaretto

Fragole al Zabaglione

Wines:

With the Antipasto—Barbera d'Asti, Bersano, 1976

With the Pasta—Corvo Bianco Salaparuta, Corvo, 1980

With the Pollo al Amaretto—Amarone Regioto della Valpolicella,
Masi, 1975

With the Zabaglione—Asti Spumanti, Cinzano
or
Sta. Kristina Antinori

Philip Roberts and Peter Mihajlov, Owners

Wayne Kostrowski, Associate Manager

Wayne Skjelstad, Executive Chef

PRONTO RISTORANTE

Restaurateurs Phil Roberts and Peter Mihajlov, well satisfied with the success of Muffuletta, their little bijou in St. Paul, were eager to expand their repertoire. So they visited many of the nation's well-known dining establishments, searching for a first-rate restaurant concept for the eighties. They found it in New York's Pronto. One look at its open-to-view pasta kitchen and they knew that they had to have one of their own. "The electricity of that room—we fell in love with it," falling also for the chrome-on-white, high-tech ambiance and genuine Italian cuisine. Six months later, having won over the proprietors of the New York Pronto, and having passed their on-site Minneapolis inspection, they were licensed to operate the only Pronto in the world. The name and the concept became theirs, along with the freedom to develop an authentic Italian statement of their own. "On that we will never compromise," vows Phil. "We insist on two things: quality and authenticity.

"We designed the menu to take people through a progression of courses, Italian style," and authentic Italian it is. Begin with antipasti—melone con prosciutto, a seafood medley, or perhaps an insalata arugula. Next a hearty bowl of minestrone or the daintier, egg-rich stracciatella; or forego that for endless variations on the pasta theme. Then, entrées feature seafood, chicken, and veal prepared in the delicate Northern Italian style. "It was tempting to build a menu for the convention crowd and include a T-bone and porterhouse," Phil reflects, "but we're standing by our statement." Consequently, a palate-cleansing sorbetto replaces the customary American baked potato and french fries.

"Pronto's not a suburban concept," says Phil of its home in the second level of the Hyatt Regency Hotel. "It's upbeat. We knew we wanted to be downtown." The pasta kitchen's tiled walls, floors, and glossy chairs in test-lab white face the glassed-in panorama of the courtyard promenade, which continues on past Pronto's more formal dining area. This room is decorated in muted tones, with lights a soft apricot color, with mirrored walls forming a backdrop to the room's centerpiece, an open oven filled with crusty loaves of bread. "In Italy, dining never will be separated from art," Phil comments. "There's a spirit that's involved, and it's a lifestyle we try to capture here." They succeed on all counts in that effort.

Hyatt Regency Hotel
1300 Nicollet Mall
Minneapolis

ANTIPASTO DI MARE RIVIERASCO

½ cup white wine
12 littleneck clams, washed
6 mussels, scrubbed
   and debearded
12 large shrimp, shelled,
   deveined, and heads
   removed

6 ounces squid
¾ pound sea scallops
1 cup MARINARA SAUCE
   Salt and pepper
1 cup chopped parsley
2 lemons, each cut in
   6 wedges

1. Pour the wine into a sauté pan. Heat over medium heat until simmering. Add the clams and mussels; cover and poach until they open, approximately 2 minutes. Discard any that do not open. Add the shrimp, squid, and scallops and continue to poach until the shrimp start to turn opaque, approximately 1 minute.
2. Add the Marinara Sauce and salt and pepper to taste. Simmer an additional 2 minutes to blend all the flavors.
3. To serve, place in a large serving bowl or in individual serving dishes. Sprinkle with the chopped parsley and garnish with the lemon wedges.

MARINARA SAUCE

¼ cup good-quality
   virgin olive oil
1 clove garlic, chopped
1 (2-pound) can whole
   Italian plum tomatoes,
   peeled

1 tablespoon chopped fresh
   basil or pinch of
   dried basil
Pinch of sugar
Salt and pepper to taste

1. Heat the oil in a saucepan over medium heat. When hot, add the garlic and brown lightly, approximately 1 to 2 minutes; do not burn.
2. In a bowl, crush the tomatoes by hand. Add the tomatoes and their juice, the basil, sugar, and salt and pepper to the saucepan; lower heat and simmer for 15 to 20 minutes, or until the sauce is reduced but still loose and runny.

We're dedicated to being absolutely authentic. Italian names precede the English ones on our menu. A language specialist led us through the pronunciation of the Italian alphabet.

PASTA PRIMAVERA

1 medium-size bunch
    broccoli, cut in florets
1 medium-size head
    cauliflower, cut in florets
1 large zucchini, halved and
    sliced into ¼"
    julienne strips
2 medium-size carrots,
    halved and sliced into
    ¼" julienne strips
½ pound green beans, cut
    in 1" pieces

2 red bell peppers, cut
    vertically in ¼" strips
½ cup fresh peas (optional)
1 teaspoon salt
1 pound fresh egg fettucine
1 quart ALFREDO SAUCE
¼ cup freshly grated
    Parmigiano Reggiano
    cheese

1. Place the broccoli florets in a saucepan and add water to cover. Blanch over medium heat approximately 5 minutes. Drain, reserving cooking liquid. Plunge into cold water to refresh. Using separate pans, repeat with the cauliflower florets, zucchini, carrots, green beans, pepper, and peas, again reserving the cooking liquid.

2. In a large bowl, thoroughly combine the blanched vegetables and refrigerate at least 1 hour or overnight, if desired.

3. In a large stockpot, place the reserved vegetable liquid with water to obtain at least 5 quarts. Bring to a rapid boil. Add the salt and then the fettucine. Stir well with a fork to separate the noodles. Cook the pasta 2 to 3 minutes or until al dente. The fresh pasta will cook quickly and float to the top when it is al dente. Immediately remove from water with a pronged wooden spoon. Drain and keep warm.

4. In a separate saucepan, warm the Alfredo Sauce over low heat for 2 to 3 minutes. Add the chilled vegetables and simmer for 3 to 4 minutes to allow the flavors of the vegetables to penetrate the sauce. Add the pasta and toss to mix. Allow to heat thoroughly over medium heat for 5 minutes.

5. To serve, place in individual bowls or on a large serving platter, stirring to arrange vegetables on top of the pasta for a pretty presentation. At the table pass the Parmigiano Reggiano for each diner to serve himself.

PRONTO RISTORANTE

ALFREDO SAUCE

1 quart *whipping cream*
½ *pound freshly grated*
   Parmigiano Reggiano
   cheese

2 *tablespoons butter*
3 *egg yolks*
   Pinch of white pepper
   Pinch of nutmeg

1. In the top pan of a double boiler, heat the cream over simmering water. When hot, add the cheese a little at a time, stirring until incorporated. Add the butter and remove from heat.
2. Stirring rapidly, slowly add the egg yolks to thicken the sauce. Season with the pepper and nutmeg.

We think this will be the restaurant of the eighties—a chic setting, pleasant service, and good food that doesn't cost an arm and a leg to enjoy.

PETTO DI POLLO AL AMARETTO

6 (½-pound) chicken breasts,
    deboned and skinned
¼ cup butter
¼ cup flour
    Salt and pepper
    Pinch of tarragon
    (optional)

1 leek, coarsely chopped
⅓ cup amaretto
1 tablespoon brandy
    (optional)
3 egg yolks
¼ cup whipping cream

1. Flatten the chicken breasts by pounding lightly between two sheets of waxed paper. In a large sauté pan, melt the butter over medium heat. Meanwhile, lightly dredge the chicken breasts in the flour; shake off excess and place in the heated pan. Season with salt and pepper to taste and add the tarragon for extra flavor, if desired. Sauté the chicken 3 to 5 minutes on each side until golden. Remove the chicken to a platter and keep warm.

2. Add the leek to the pan and sauté until limp, approximately 4 minutes.

3. Add the amaretto to the pan to deglaze, stirring briskly for 1 to 2 minutes. After deglazing with the amaretto, add the brandy if desired. While stirring, flame the mixture so that the alcohol will burn off. Reduce heat to a simmer.

4. In a small bowl, mix the egg yolks and the cream and add to the pan mixture, stirring constantly. Return the chicken to the pan and simmer over low heat for 2 to 3 minutes until the sauce thickens. Place the chicken on the serving platter and pour the sauce over. Serve at once.

People come back often, so it's important to keep the menu fresh, alive, and original.

FRAGOLE AL ZABAGLIONE

1 *quart fresh strawberries, washed, hulled, and halved*	15 *egg yolks* 1 *cup sugar* 1½ *cups Marsala wine*

1. Place the strawberries into six individual dessert dishes or glasses.
2. In the top of a double boiler over simmering water, combine the egg yolks and the sugar to make the sauce. Stir slowly but constantly over low heat 6 to 8 minutes until the mixture begins to thicken. Be sure the heat is very low so the eggs will not scramble.
3. As the eggs begin to thicken, gradually add the Marsala until all is incorporated. Do not stir vigorously; air should not be whipped into the sauce. Remove the top of the double boiler from the heat at any time, if the sauce appears to be getting too hot. Pour the warm, thick sauce over the strawberries and serve.

This sauce is also very good over fresh raspberries, blueberries, or used as a custard filling in torte and cakes. If you use it in a cake or torte, you should fold in an equal amount of sweetened whipped cream.

SCHUMACHER'S NEW PRAGUE HOTEL

Dinner for Six

Goulash Soup

Chicken with Mushrooms in Cream Gravy

Potato Dumplings

Sautéed Red Cabbage

Creamed Green Peas

Smoked Herring Salad

Fruit Cream Dessert

Beverages:

A dry white wine
or
Pilsner Urquell Czechoslovakian beer

John Schumacher, Proprietor and Chef

SCHUMACHER'S NEW PRAGUE HOTEL

It was a Tuesday, John Schumacher remembers, eight years ago, when he and his wife Nancy discovered a gracious, turn-of-the-century red brick hotel. They had travelled 40 miles south of the Twin Cities to the Czech and German community of New Prague, and returned Wednesday morning to sign purchase papers. Restoration of Schumacher's New Prague Hotel began soon after. Several trips to Europe for antiques, as well as for menu ideas, established the theme, and the hotel was furnished like a middle-European inn. From the lobby to the tiny barroom to the guest apartments above, each room was decorated with impeccable attention to detail—hand-painted leaded windows, for example, or wooden settees, Salzburg linen wallpaper, and Bavarian floral folk art. In this magnificent setting, a restaurant planned with as much care boasts a cuisine which features some fifty authentic Czech and German dishes.

The menu is both outstanding and authentic in its style. "Everything is made from scratch, from local products," proprietor-chef John advises. "We cut our own veal, make our own cucumber pickles, season our own sausages, get flour from the local mill, and butter from the creamery." The dedication is apparent in the excellence of the food, as well as on the guests' faces: no one leaves the New Prague Hotel hungry.

Generous servings of homemade soups and the salad platter's marinated vegetables awaken the appetite, to be then pleased by schnitzels, rouladen, and well-seasoned Czech sausages. Many game dishes can then further delight, entrées such as quail stuffed with plums and wrapped in bacon, pheasant with mushrooms and shallots, or rabbit roasted with caraway and sauced in heavy cream. The accompaniments are Old World—knedliky dumplings, fresh spätzle noodles, sauerkraut, red cabbage, fresh rye rolls, and sweet poppyseed kolacky buns. The sauces are rich in cream and butter and aromatically seasoned with wine and caraway. If a diner is not sated by all this, a choice like Czech-style cheesecake, apple strudel, or Honza's Torte—a mountainous dessert of meringue, chopped nuts, whipped cream, and chocolate—could surely change that.

212 West Main Street
New Prague

SCHUMACHER'S NEW PRAGUE HOTEL

GOULASH SOUP

2 onions, chopped
¼ cup plus 2 tablespoons butter
¼ teaspoon paprika
1 pound chuck or shank beef, cut in 1" cubes
¼ cup flour
½ cup coarsely chopped carrot

½ cup coarsely chopped parsnip
½ cup coarsely chopped celery
Salt to taste
1 pound potatoes, peeled and coarsely chopped
¼ teaspoon caraway seeds
Dash of pepper

1. In a heavy stockpot, fry the onions in the 2 tablespoons butter until limp. Add the paprika and beef. Cook slowly until brown, about 30 minutes.
2. Melt the remaining ¼ cup butter; blend in the flour and fry until golden, stirring constantly. Add to the stockpot with 1½ quarts boiling water. Add the carrot, parsnip, celery, and salt, stirring to mix. Simmer for 20 minutes.
3. Add the potatoes, caraway seeds, and pepper. Simmer until potatoes are tender, about 20 to 30 minutes. Serve hot.

The hotel is listed in Country Inns and Back Roads *and in Europe's* Romantik Hotels und Restaurants — *the first American inn to be included, which makes me proud!*

CHICKEN WITH MUSHROOMS IN CREAM GRAVY

2 *small chickens, cut up*
½ *cup butter*
1 *large onion, chopped*
1 *cup mushrooms, wiped*
   clean and sliced

Salt to taste
1 *cup sour cream*
1 *tablespoon flour*

1. In a large heavy frying pan, brown the chicken in the butter, turning frequently. Add the onion. Cook 3 minutes, stirring frequently until wilted. Add the mushrooms, salt, and 1½ cups water. Cover and simmer until tender, about 45 minutes. Remove chicken from pan and keep warm while making gravy.
2. Mix the sour cream and the flour in a small bowl; blend into the pan juices, whisking constantly until the gravy boils. Pour over the chicken, and serve at once.

I said to myself, "when I have a hotel of my own, I want to do it right." I run this business on energy, sixteen hours a day of it. Living right on the premises keeps me on top of everything.

POTATO DUMPLINGS

2 *pounds potatoes, peeled*
   Salt to taste

1 *egg*
3 *cups flour*

1. Coarsely grate the potatoes; drain on paper towels and pat dry.
2. Place in a bowl with the salt, egg, and flour. Mix well.
3. Drop by large spoonfuls into a large pot of boiling, salted water. Cook 6 to 8 minutes, making sure the dumplings do not stick to the bottom of the pot. Remove with a skimmer and serve hot with the chicken.

Every entrée is fresh and prepared to order. It may take a bit longer, but it tastes so much better.

SAUTÉED RED CABBAGE

1½ pounds red cabbage,
   coarsely shredded
½ cup lard
1 medium-size onion,
   chopped

½ teaspoon caraway seeds
  Salt to taste
1 to 2 teaspoons sugar
  Juice of 1 lemon
2 teaspoons flour

1. Place 1 cup water in a stockpot. Add the cabbage and simmer for about 5 minutes.
2. Heat the lard in a small skillet; add the onion and sauté until brown. Add to the cabbage along with the caraway seeds and salt; sauté 10 to 15 minutes.
3. Add the sugar, lemon juice, and flour, whisking so that flour does not lump. Simmer for 5 minutes. Serve at once with the chicken.

Note: Vinegar may be substituted for the lemon juice. Use according to personal taste.

All side dishes—and main courses and desserts—are made from fresh produce from the area's nearby farms.

CREAMED GREEN PEAS

1 pound fresh green peas
   (approximately 2 cups)
¼ cup butter
½ teaspoon sugar
  Salt to taste

  Pepper to taste
  Dash of nutmeg
1 cup whipping cream
2 tablespoons flour
1 tablespoon minced parsley

1. Simmer the peas in ½ cup boiling, salted water for 5 minutes. Drain.
2. Heat the butter in a skillet and add the sugar. Add the peas and sauté for 5 to 10 minutes, or until tender. Stir in the salt, pepper, and nutmeg.
3. Stir the cream and the flour together in a small bowl; stir into the peas. Simmer for 3 minutes. Before serving, add the parsley. Serve hot with the chicken.

SCHUMACHER'S NEW PRAGUE HOTEL

SMOKED HERRING SALAD

½ pound smoked herring,
   boned and coarsely diced
½ pound potatoes, cooked,
   peeled, and coarsely diced
1 small onion, chopped

1 cup mayonnaise
  Lemon juice to taste
6 large, cup-shaped leaves
  iceberg lettuce

Combine all ingredients except the lettuce. Mound the herring mixture in the lettuce cups just before serving.

Note: The herring mixture may be prepared several hours in advance and refrigerated.

When my grandpa heard that I wanted to be a cook, he thought I was nuts—but he gave me some advice. He said to me, "if you want to feed 'em kid, feed 'em good grub." And that's what I try to do.

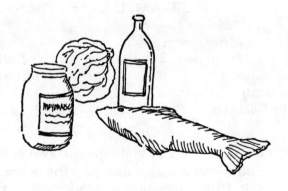

FRUIT CREAM DESSERT

1 cup milk
2 egg yolks
¼ cup sugar
1 tablespoon cornstarch
2 tablespoons cognac
1 cup whipping cream,
    whipped until stiff

⅔ cup chopped toasted nuts
1 orange, thinly sliced
½ cup candied cherries,
    halved
½ cup green grapes

Mix together the milk, egg yolks, sugar, and cornstarch in a small pan. Over medium heat, bring to a full boil, stirring constantly. Cool to room temperature. Add the cognac and 1 cup of the whipped cream, folding gently. Fold in the nuts, orange, candied cherries, and grapes. Pour into a mold or serving bowl and chill several hours or overnight, until firm. Just before serving, decorate with the remaining 1 cup whipped cream.

Our breads and pastries are prepared fresh daily, and the ingredients are always the best we can get.

Dinner for Six

Oysters Rockefeller

Fishmarket Chowder

Shipside Salad

Sole Semiramis

Tarte au Citron

Wine:

Mâconnais, Mâcon-Villages, Bouchard Père et Fils

Blaine Wilkinson, General Manager

Pierre-Jean Laupies, Executive Chef

SHIPSIDE

Pierre-Jean Laupies, executive chef of the Radisson South Hotel's Shipside restaurant, was raised in Nîmes, France, where he played in the kitchen long before he worked there. "In my country, cooking is like a religion. I didn't play with toys, I played with a griddle stove." That is, until age fourteen when he was apprenticed to the highly reputed Prunier's of Paris. He then served at London's Maxim's, the Savoy, Mayfair's Mirabelle, as cruise chef for a Mediterranean tour bearing six hundred passengers, and in Guadaloupe and the French West Indies, before becoming executive chef for the Rosewood Room in Minneapolis. In April, 1981, he assumed his current position. With this extensive and diverse background, Pierre-Jean is clear about what is his forte in the business: "What I like to do is hotel business. That's what I do best. And what I am most interested in cooking is fish."

It is to the the benefit of Minneapolis diners that Jean-Pierre's preference is such, because before his arrival in the city, they did not even recognize the distinction of fresh seafood. "When I came to Minneapolis seven years ago," he says, "you couldn't find fresh fish here at all. 'People don't know the difference,' they told me." Under his tutelage, they now do. His appetizer menu offers fresh mussels, oysters, escargot, and a special gravlaks dish. The entrées—all made with fresh ingredients—include such courses as snapper in an Oriental ginger sauce; sole or halibut poached with shallots, wine, and cream; and shrimp on a bed of alfalfa served with a side dish of sweet-sour sauce. The vegetable accompaniments, julienned and cooked al dente, are carefully selected to provide color and texture contrast.

To complement the exquisite specialty of the cuisine, Shipside is decorated like a seafaring vessel. The restaurant's rough walls are hung with ship wheels, lobster crates, ropes, nets, and other well-worn fishing gear, while tableside aquariums establish an undersea tranquility. Miniature ships' lanterns and seagreen runners on the tables are in keeping with the pewter dinner plates. Then, the serving and kitchen staff is as skilled as any ship's crew, with Jean-Pierre functioning as captain: "What I say is what I want to get. Either they work for me, or they're out. They've all got to be good—or they wouldn't be here." That's the kind of tight ship that produces smooth sailing at Shipside.

Radisson South Hotel
Highway 100 and I-494
Bloomington

SHIPSIDE

OYSTERS ROCKEFELLER

3 packages frozen chopped
    spinach, thawed
2 tablespoons butter
3 medium-size shallots,
    very finely chopped
½ cup Pernod
½ teaspoon salt
⅛ teaspoon pepper

MORNAY SAUCE
2 dozen oysters on the
    half-shell, freshly
    opened
3 tablespoons shredded
    Swiss cheese
3 tablespoons shredded
    cheddar cheese

1. Squeeze most of the water from the spinach. In a sauté pan, melt the butter. Add the shallots and cook them over medium heat until transparent, approximately 5 minutes. Add the spinach and cook for 10 minutes. Add the Pernod, salt, pepper, and approximately one-third of the Mornay Sauce; simmer over low heat for 5 minutes. Correct the seasonings, then remove the spinach from the heat and let cool.
2. Preheat oven to 375°.
3. Arrange the oysters on rock salt divided among six individual oven-proof dishes. Cover each oyster with spinach and place in preheated oven for 10 to 15 minutes. Remove from the oven and preheat broiler. Top each dish with the remaining Mornay Sauce. Sprinkle with the shredded Swiss and cheddar cheeses and place under the broiler to glaze, approximately 1 to 2 minutes. Serve immediately.

MORNAY SAUCE

1½ cups milk
1 tablespoon flour
10 ounces aged Swiss
    cheese, shredded

¼ teaspoon salt
Dash of white pepper
2 egg yolks

In a saucepan, bring the milk to a boil. Make a roux by blending the flour and 1 tablespoon water. Add the roux to the milk and whisk over low heat until smooth. Add the cheese, salt, and pepper. Simmer for 10 minutes. Let cool slightly. Beat the egg yolks slightly and stir into the sauce.

The critics as well as the customers rave over this dish. "Every restaurant in town should have this recipe," they tell me.

FISH MARKET CHOWDER

¼ pound white fish
¼ cup butter
2 small onions, diced
¼ head celery, diced
⅛ teaspoon saffron
¼ cup flour
¾ cup canned clam juice
1 teaspoon all-purpose seasoning salt
½ teaspoon salt

¼ teaspoon white pepper
2 teaspoons dry granules of chicken bouillon
¼ pound salad shrimp
¼ pound baby scallops
2 ounces snow crabmeat, coarsely cut
¼ pound shucked clams with juice

1. Poach the fish in 1 cup boiling water. Reduce heat and simmer, uncovered, until tender. Cut the fish in chunks and set aside with its liquid.
2. In a large sauté pan, melt the butter and sauté the onions, celery, and saffron over medium heat until transparent, approximately 5 minutes. Stir the flour into ¼ cup cold water to make a roux. Add to the sautéed mixture, stirring, and cook 15 to 20 minutes over medium low heat. Do not allow to brown.
3. Add the clam juice and 1 quart water; stir well. Add the seasoning salt, salt, white pepper, chicken bouillon, fish with liquid, shrimp, scallops, crabmeat, and clams. Bring to a slow boil. Simmer until the roux has cooked well into the stock, approximately 20 minutes. Correct seasonings if necessary and serve.

This soup is a real trademark of the Radisson Hotels, and many of our customers order it as their main course

SHIPSIDE SALAD

1 head iceberg lettuce,
  coarsely torn
¼ pound mushrooms, sliced
  (approximately)
6 canned artichoke bottoms,
  cut in half vertically
10 radishes, sliced
3 tablespoons chopped
  walnuts

¾ cup *VILTOFT DRESSING*
  (approximately)
2 tomatoes, each cut
  in 6 wedges
2 hard-boiled eggs, each
  cut in 6 wedges

In a large bowl, mix the lettuce, mushrooms, artichokes, radishes, and walnuts. Toss with the Viltoft Dressing. Top with the tomato and egg and serve immediately.

VILTOFT DRESSING

2 egg yolks
1 (1-pound) jar mayonnaise
¾ cup buttermilk
¼ cup grated Parmesan
  cheese
1½ cups salad oil
3 tablespoons vinegar
1 tablespoon plus 1½
  teaspoons lemon juice

¼ teaspoon dry mustard
¾ teaspoon Worcestershire
  sauce
1 drop Tabasco sauce
1 drop liquid garlic
¼ teaspoon freshly ground
  pepper
Dash of salt

1. In a small bowl of electric mixer, whip the eggs into the mayonnaise at low speed. Add the buttermilk and cheese. Increase mixer speed and slowly add the oil, beating until it is fully incorporated.

2. Reduce the mixer speed and add the vinegar, lemon juice, mustard, Worcestershire sauce, Tabasco sauce, garlic, pepper, and salt. Reserve about ¾ cup dressing for the Shipside Salad and refrigerate the remainder.

Note: This dressing can be made ahead and refrigerated until needed.

After three years of getting up in the cold and dark to scrub vegetables, wash pots, and light fires, I passed my qualifying exams in France and went on to serve as officers' chef in the army. The way I was trained is the way I operate in the kitchen today: what I say is what I want to get. It took the staff a while to adjust, but now they are excited to work here and proud to do a good job.

SOLE SEMIRAMIS

6 (6-ounce) lemon sole
   fillets
1 cup flour
½ teaspoon salt
¼ teaspoon white pepper
1 egg, lightly beaten
4 tablespoons butter
¼ cup oil

CREAMED MUSHROOMS
WILD RICE RADISSON
   (see second page following)
¼ cup toasted almonds
3 tablespoons chopped
   parsley
3 lemons

1. Divide the fillets into two strips each, cutting lengthwise. Mix the flour with the salt and pepper and dredge the fish in the mixture. Combine the egg with 1 tablespoon water and stir to mix. Dip the floured fillets in this egg wash.

2. In a large skillet, melt the butter over low heat; remove the butter's milky sediment and discard. Add the oil to the clarified butter and sauté the fillets over medium heat until golden and flaky, testing after 3 minutes.

3. Place the Creamed Mushrooms on one side of a large serving platter; then place the sautéed fish on top of the mushrooms. Place the Wild Rice Radisson on the opposite side of the plate. Sprinkle with toasted almonds and parsley. Cut the lemons in half and add as garnish. Serve at once.

SHIPSIDE

CREAMED MUSHROOMS

¾ pound plus 2 tablespoons
   butter
5 tablespoons diced onion
2 tablespoons chopped
   shallots
2 pounds mushrooms,
   washed and sliced

2 tablespoons flour
1½ quarts White Fish Stock
   (see index)
1½ cups white wine
½ teaspoon salt
¼ teaspoon white pepper

1. In a 2-quart casserole, heat ¾ pound butter and sauté the onion and shallots over medium heat until golden, approximately 5 minutes. Add the mushrooms; stir and sauté about 3 minutes.
2. Make a roux by mixing the remaining 2 tablespoons butter and the flour. In a saucepan, warm the fish stock and whisk in the roux. Cook over medium heat 20 minutes, or until reduced by half. Add with the wine to the casserole and simmer about 3 minutes over low heat. Season with the salt and pepper, and serve hot.

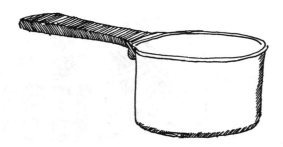

SHIPSIDE

WILD RICE RADISSON

6 cups wild rice

2 pounds mushrooms,
  washed and sliced

2 quarts canned beef
  consommé

3 cups diced celery

3 cups diced onion

6 cups butter

Mix all ingredients together in a Dutch oven and let stand for 3 hours. Bake in 325° oven for 1½ hours, covered.

This entrée is the perfect blend of a native Minnesota product and fresh Boston seafood.

Both the style of purveying and the method of cooking seafood has changed dramatically in the seven years I've been in Minnesota. Now we're serving fresh escargot, fresh mussels, European fish. I've taken the idea of a London broil and made a mixed grill of seafood instead. On the lunch menu there's even a fish Reuben and a seafood club sandwich!

TARTE AU CITRON

3 large lemons
3 eggs
1½ cups sugar

1 cup whipping cream
PÂTE SABLÉ

1. Preheat oven to 300°.
2. Grate the rinds off the lemons and reserve. Squeeze the lemons and set the juice aside.
3. Break the eggs into a small bowl. Add the sugar and beat until thick and lemon-colored, approximately 5 minutes.
4. Whip the cream until soft peaks form. Fold into the egg/sugar mixture. Add the reserved lemon juice and rind and fold just to blend.
5. Roll out the Pâte Sablé on a pastry board; cut a circle 10 inches in diameter. Line a 9-inch pie pan with the dough and flute the edges. Pour the lemon filling into the pie dough and bake in preheated oven for 45 minutes.

PÂTE SABLÉ

2 eggs, lightly beaten
1¾ cups butter
½ cup sugar

2 cups flour
1 to 3 tablespoons whipping
cream

1. With an electric beater, beat the eggs one at a time into the butter until thoroughly combined. Add the sugar and beat until smooth.
2. With a fork, cut in the flour and as much of the cream as needed to permit the mixture to be gathered into a ball. Form a ball and refrigerate the dough at least ½ hour, or until thoroughly chilled.

This isn't like any lemon pie you've had before. It's fantastic: light and refreshing—just a great dish!

Dinner for Six

Chilled Shrimp and Buttermilk Soup

Stuffed Pasta Shells with Saffron Sauce

Chicken and Hazelnut Mousse

Red Snapper en Croûte

Insalata Fantasia Belga

Chestnut Mousse

Wines:

With the Pasta Shells—Corvo, Duca de Salaparuta, 1979
With the Mousse—Gancia, Pinot di Pinot NV
With the Red Snapper—Pinot Bianco, S. Margherita, 1979

Fred Corso, General Manager
Jan Peacock, Director of Food and Beverages
Bruce Caron, Executive Chef

STRADIVARIUS

Stradivarius, the formal dining room of the Sheraton Ritz Hotel, is an expression of imagination and dedication to fine dining. The Northern Italian menu marries classic and nouvelle cuisine in an unusual and delightful way. Tuscany favorites such as seafod, veal, and fresh herbs seem newly born when prepared with Stradivarius's sauces: mussels simmered with white wine and anise, sea bass steamed with fennel, lamb cooked in juniper and gin. "There are no shortcuts with our sauces," declares Executive Chef Bruce Caron. For example, nearly a hundred pounds of veal bones form the basis for the fifty gallons of stock which are brought down to two quarts of veal demi-glace. The chef further comments that "all our sauces are flourless reductions, finished with sweet butter. It's incredibly expensive, what we do—white wine, fennel, saffron, truffles, double cream—but the diner deserves it. We give people not just vegetables, but exciting vegetables they couldn't get before. It gets tiresome to see carrots on your plate all the time."

A small lounge off the hotel's lobby sets the tone of subtle elegance that extends to the restaurant. Dark wood paneling, soft lights, and a few potted palms reflect the forest green of the room's banquettes. Chairs of plush burgundy circle the well-spaced tables with their tasteful appointments of German linens set with heavy silver bearing the Stradivarius violin-scroll motif, tiny table lamps, and miniature bouquets. Classic simplicity: "Not a lot of distraction, because the most important element is the food," avers Jan Peacock, British-born and internationally trained director of food and beverages.

He has schooled his staff well in the European-style plate service, increased their knowledge of food and wine, and even given them a familiarity with the Italian language favored on the menu. And he takes pride in the cellar book he has compiled, an international blend of Italian, French, and California labels. The evening concludes with a complimentary glass of sambuca with an amaretto cookie, another Stradivarius touch of class.

Sheraton Ritz Hotel
315 Nicollet Mall
Minneapolis

STRADIVARIUS

CHILLED SHRIMP AND BUTTERMILK SOUP

2 pounds medium-size shrimp, shelled and deveined	1 teaspoon sugar
	1 teaspoon dry mustard
1½ teaspoons salt	½ teaspoon ground cumin
3 tablespoons chopped fresh dill	¼ teaspoon pepper
	2 medium-size cucumbers
	1½ quarts buttermilk

1. In a large saucepan, bring 1 quart water to boil. Add the shrimp and 1 teaspoon of the salt and return to boiling. Cook the shrimp until tender, approximately 1½ minutes. Drain, cool, and mince.
2. In a large bowl, combine the shrimp, 2 tablespoons of the dill, the sugar, mustard, cumin, the remaining ½ teaspoon salt, and the pepper. Let stand 30 minutes.
3. Peel the cucumbers; cut in half lengthwise and then into thin slices. Add to the shrimp mixture; toss. Stir in the buttermilk and refrigerate, covered, until chilled.
4. Serve in individual bowls with a garnish of the remaining dill.

We grow our own fresh herbs for the garnish.

STRADIVARIUS

STUFFED PASTA SHELLS WITH SAFFRON SAUCE

1¼ teaspoons salt
1 pound jumbo pasta shells
½ cup plus 1 teaspoon butter
¼ pound medium-size
   shrimp, shelled and
   deveined
¼ pound scallops
¼ pound crabmeat
¼ pound halibut or other
   firm-fleshed fish,
   deboned and skinned

1 teaspoon flour
½ cup milk
  Pepper to taste
½ cup freshly grated
   Parmesan cheese
  SAFFRON SAUCE

1. In a large saucepan, bring 2 quarts water to boil. Add 1 teaspoon of the salt and the pasta shells. Cook 7 minutes, or until al dente. Immerse the shells in ice water to halt the cooking process. Drain and reserve.
2. Melt ½ cup butter in a sauté pan over medium heat. Sauté the shrimp, scallops, crabmeat, and halibut until just tender, approximately 6 to 8 minutes. In a food processor or with a sharp knife, finely chop all the seafood. Set aside.
3. Preheat oven to 350°.
4. In a small saucepan, make a roux by mixing the flour with the remaining 1 teaspoon butter. Whisk in the milk, remaining ¼ teaspoon salt and pepper; simmer over low heat for 3 minutes until the sauce thickens. Remove from heat and add the chopped seafood. Mix well to bind.
5. Fill the reserved pasta shells with the seafood/cream mixture, using a spoon. Place the stuffed shells on a baking sheet and sprinkle with the Parmesan cheese. Bake in preheated oven 15 minutes, or until heated through. Serve on individual plates with Saffron Sauce passed in a sauceboat.

SAFFRON SAUCE

6 tablespoons white wine
  Pinch of saffron
1 cup whipping cream

1 cup unsalted butter
  Salt and pepper

1. In a sauté pan over medium heat, place the wine and the saffron and simmer for 2 to 3 minutes. Add the cream and bring to a boil; lower heat and reduce by half, approximately 5 minutes. Remove from heat.
2. Add the butter one pat at a time, while swirling the pan. Season with salt and pepper to taste.

The Northern Italian cuisine of Stradivarius emphasizes seafoods, veal, and natural sauces. We spend a large amount of time on presentation.

CHICKEN AND HAZELNUT MOUSSE

3 (½-pound) chicken breasts,
  deboned and skinned
2 egg whites
½ cup chopped hazelnuts
1 teaspoon dried sage

Salt and pepper to taste
1 cup whipping cream
4 cups Chicken Stock
  (see index)
HERBED TOMATO SAUCE
  (see next page)

1. In a food processor, combine the chicken breasts and the egg whites to form a paste. Add the nuts, sage, and salt and pepper. Add the cream slowly and process until the consistency of smooth paste. Cool.
2. Meanwhile, pour the chicken stock into a saucepan and bring to a simmer over medium heat. Shape the cooled chicken mixture into 2-inch oval dumplings and drop several at a time into the chicken stock. Simmer about 5 minutes. Remove with a slotted spoon and drain on paper towels. Keep warm while cooking the remaining dumplings.
3. Serve immediately on individual plates. Top each serving with Herbed Tomato Sauce.

The influence of nouvelle cuisine is felt today in Northern Italy. We prefer to keep away from the well-known dishes here and perfect other ventures.

HERBED TOMATO SAUCE

1 cup Chicken Stock
  (see index)
¼ cup tomato paste
½ cup whipping cream

¼ cup white wine
½ teaspoon dried sage
¼ pound unsalted butter,
  sliced

Combine all ingredients except the butter in a saucepan. Bring to a boil over medium heat and reduce by half, or until the sauce coats the back of a wooden spoon, approximately 5 minutes. Remove from heat and swirl the butter slices into the sauce.

RED SNAPPER EN CROÛTE

1 pound salmon
3 egg whites
3 cups whipping cream
  Dash of nutmeg
  Salt
  Pepper
½ pound broccoli florets
  (approximately 2 cups)

1 teaspoon lemon juice
2 sheets frozen puff
  pastry, thawed
1 (½ to ¾-pound) fillet
  of red snapper
1 egg
  SORREL SAUCE

1. In a food processor, process the salmon and two of the egg whites to a paste. Chill a few minutes. Put the mixture in a bowl and beat in 2 cups of the cream, stirring until thick and smooth. Add the nutmeg, ¼ teaspoon salt, and a pinch of pepper. Refrigerate until ready to use.

2. In a saucepan, bring 2 cups of water to boil; add the broccoli and blanch for 5 minutes. Refresh in ice water; drain. Process the broccoli and remaining egg white in the food processor. Chill a few minutes, then place in a bowl and beat in the remaining 1 cup cream, the lemon juice, ¼ teaspoon salt, and a pinch of pepper. Chill until ready to use.

3. On a cookie sheet with a 1-inch rim, spread flat one sheet of the puff pastry, keeping the other sheet covered with a damp towel. Lay the snapper fillet on the puff pastry, leaving plenty of border. Spread the salmon mousse in a ¾-inch-thick layer over the top of the fillet, making a dome shape in the center. Mold the broccoli mousse on top of the salmon mousse.

4. Preheat oven to 400°.

5. Beat the egg with a pinch of salt and brush this egg wash around the fillet on the pastry. Lay the second sheet of pastry over the layered fillet. Using your hands, shape the pastry into an oval sphere, pressing the two sheets together to join edges. Cut off all but a ½-inch border of pastry and tuck this border underneath the oval. Use the scraps to make a fish tail and head and attach by brushing with egg wash and pressing to adhere.

6. Bake in preheated oven for 20 minutes. When baked, remove and let rest 5 minutes. Slice vertically into six portions and serve on individual plates, accompanied with the Sorrel Sauce.

SORREL SAUCE

1 teaspoon salt	Dash of lemon juice
2½ cups fresh sorrel	Salt and pepper to taste
¼ cup white wine	½ cup unsalted butter, sliced
1 cup whipping cream	

1. In a saucepan, heat 2 cups water to boiling. Add the salt and blanch the sorrel in the boiling water until it turns bright green, approximately 5 minutes. Refresh the sorrel in ice water; drain and purée in an electric blender.

2. In a saucepan, place the white wine and the cream and boil over medium heat until reduced by half, approximately 5 minutes. Add the sorrel purée, lemon juice, and salt and pepper. Remove from heat. Swirl in the butter slices, whisking until incorporated.

We use the best products procurable, the freshest. Our snapper comes from Boston. I come from New England myself, and I do like to work with fish!

STRADIVARIUS

INSALATA FANTASIA BELGA

2 heads Boston lettuce,
 rinsed
1 bunch watercress
 (approximately 2 cups)
2 Belgian endives, rinsed
3 large ripe tomatoes

2 cups walnut oil
1 cup fresh lemon juice
½ teaspoon salt
¼ teaspoon pepper
1 tablespoon finely chopped
 fresh tarragon

1. Divide the Boston lettuce between six individual large salad plates. Place the watercress on top of the lettuce.
2. Cut the endives into thin vertical slices. Thinly slice the tomatoes. Alternate slices of the endive and the tomato on top of the salads.
3. In a small bowl, blend the oil, lemon juice, salt, pepper, and tarragon. Drizzle evenly over the salads just before serving.

Note: For best flavor, cover and let the dressing stand for 12 hours. Stir or shake well before using.

STRADIVARIUS

CHESTNUT MOUSSE

2 (1-pound) cans purée
  of chestnuts
1¾ cups plus 2 tablespoons
  confectioners' sugar
4 tablespoons butter,
  at room temperature

3 tablespoons kirschwasser
1½ teaspoons vanilla extract
1 cup whipping cream,
  chilled

1. In a mixing bowl, stir the chestnut purée, 1¾ cups sugar, butter, kirschwasser, and 1 teaspoon vanilla extract. Fill a pastry bag with the chestnut mixture and pipe it into six dessert glasses. Chill ½ hour or until ready to serve.
2. Beat the cream with an electric beater until it holds its shape. Add ½ teaspoon vanilla extract and fold in the remaining 2 tablespoons sugar. Just before serving, garnish each dessert with a dollop of the whipped cream.

After dessert, we serve each guest a cordial glass of sambuca con mosca: it's the thing in Northern Italy! Three coffee beans are the "mosca" flies in the liqueur.

La Tortue

Dinner for Six

Gravlaks

Crème d'Artichauts

Ris de Veau aux Épinards

Salade La Tortue

Gâteau Saint-Honoré

Wines:
With the Gravlaks—Graves, 1978
or
Chassagne-Montrachet-Côte de Beaune, 1977
With the Ris de Veau—Château Bel-Air,
St.-Émilion, Premier Grand Cru, 1976
With the Gâteau—Sainte-Croix-du-Mont, 1978
or
Taittinger, Blanc de Blancs, 1973

Tor and Kristine Aasheim, Owners

Paul Laubignat, Executive Chef

LA TORTUE

Situated in the heart of downtown Minneapolis, La Tortue's cuisine, decor, and ambiance capture the charm of a European chateau. Co-owners Tor and Kristine Aasheim are dedicated to maintaining the excellence of their dining establishment, personally monitoring such details as the placement of fresh flowers on the tables and organization of the lengthy reservations list, which generally includes the names of celebrated individuals. They are proud to have their own restaurant.

Tor trained as a chef in his native Oslo and graduated at the top of his class in Lausann's hotel academies. He toured the world several times over on Norwegian luxury liners, "in charge of everything between the bridge and rear deck," including the elegant meals demanded by discerning voyagers. But in 1968, he and his bride Kristine decided to move to America, to Minneapolis. Tor's skills were eagerly sought by hotels, clubs, and restaurants, but until La Tortue opened in April, 1981, they did not consider Minneapolis home.

They selected a lively locale in the heart of the city for La Tortue— "the turtle." They renovated an old warehouse, relying on their own good taste. "People say it looks just like our living room," smiles Kristine. Although homey and unpretentious, the furnishings are at the same time exquisite. The floral print on the walls of the foyer is repeated on the hand-carved chairs in the dining room. Brilliant mirrored columns rise above soft banquettes, creating an air of elegance. The lace curtains and chandeliers were imported from France, as were the carved entrance portal and antique armoire that houses La Tortue's vintage wines.

Like the decor, the menu is reflected in the hors d'oeuvres display of Gravlaks, herring, goose liver pâté, and fried Camembert sparked with lingonberry sauce. Both nouvelle and heartier Continental specialties of French Chef Paul Laubignat are in evidence—a garlic-seasoned mousse of escargots, duck breast salad, whole roasted chicken anointed with morels and cream, fresh eel filled with pike mousse, and sweetbreads on a spinach base. With the unusual combination of sophistication and simplicity which defines La Tortue, the menu features a special creation which honors the restaurant's name—fresh turtle soup served with tortoise-shaped croutons.

Butler Square West
100 North 6th Street
Minneapolis

GRAVLAKS

2 pounds center cut of fresh
    salmon (Atlantic, sockeye,
    coho, or Chinook)
¼ cup salt
½ cup sugar
1 bunch fresh dill, coarsely
    chopped (approximately)
1 tablespoon sherry

1 tablespoon oil
2 teaspoons crushed white
    peppercorns
1 cucumber, sliced
3 lemons, cut in wedges
   GRAVLAKS SAUCE (see
    next page)

1. Two days in advance, scale and debone the salmon, cutting the fish into two pieces along the line of the backbone. Do not rinse the pieces, but wipe them dry with paper towels. Mix the salt and the sugar and rub the fish with one-fourth of the mixture.

2. Sprinkle another one-fourth of the salt/sugar mixture and some of the dill in a deep baking dish. Place one piece of salmon in the dish skin side down and sprinkle generously with the dill, reserving the rest for garnish. Sprinkle with the sherry, oil, crushed peppercorns, and another one-fourth of the salt/sugar mixture.

3. Cover with the second piece of salmon, skin side up. If the pieces do not match in shape, place the thick side against the thin side. Sprinkle with the remaining salt/sugar mixture. Cover the dish with aluminum foil and a light weight such as a chopping board. The fish will "leach out" in 4 to 5 hours and the fluid should be poured off.

4. Refrigerate at least 48 hours, turning the salmon pieces around at least four to five times during that period. (The cured salmon can be stored in the refrigerator and, if well chilled, should keep for two to three weeks.)

5. To serve, cut into thin slices. Garnish with the sliced cucumber, remaining dill, lemon wedges, and Gravlaks Sauce.

Although recipes differ in amount of salt and sugar to use, the one-half sugar to one-quarter salt ratio is typical. I believe this proportion produces an ideal cure with only the faintest suggestion of a sweet flavor.

Any angler who has fished in Scandinavia is familiar with this raw, salt and sugar cured salmon which is featured in so many country inns. It is the pure essence of the fish and a preparation for which I have an absolute craving after a day on the river. Here we go through a whole side of salmon daily.

GRAVLAKS SAUCE

3 tablespoons oil
1 tablespoon red wine
   vinegar
1 tablespoon sugar
1 teaspoon salt
   Pinch of white pepper

3 tablespoons Dijon mustard
1 teaspoon sherry
2 tablespoons minced dill

Combine all ingredients except the dill. Add the dill and serve.

CRÈME D'ARTICHAUTS

6 large artichokes
   Juice of 1 lemon
2 tablespoons butter
1 large onion, peeled and
   coarsely chopped
2 leeks, washed, trimmed,
   and chopped

2 quarts clear Chicken
   Stock (see index)
1½ cups whipping cream
   Salt and pepper

1. With a sharp knife, cut off the stems and leaves of the artichokes and remove the chokes. Discard. Cut the artichoke hearts in quarters. Place the hearts in a bowl, add water to cover and the lemon juice.
2. Heat the butter in a stainless steel saucepan. Drain the artichoke hearts and add to the saucepan with the onion and leeks. Sauté for 2 to 3 minutes without letting them color. Add chicken stock and let cook for 30 minutes.
3. Purée the artichoke/chicken stock mixture in an electric blender. Return the purée to the saucepan and add the cream and salt and pepper to taste. Reheat gently; serve at once in individual soup bowls.

We don't want to hear, "it's good." That's not enough. We want it to be the best. The service is the way we want it—and now so is the food.

RIS DE VEAU AUX ÉPINARDS

3 clusters veal sweetbreads
3 pounds spinach, washed
2 cups dry white wine
1 leek, washed, trimmed,
    and cut in half
2 stalks celery
1 medium-size onion, cut
    in half
1 bunch dill, with stems

¼ pound plus 4 tablespoons
    lightly salted butter
1 pound mushrooms, washed
    and sliced
Salt and pepper to taste
6 tablespoons all-purpose
    flour
2 cups whipping cream
    or crème fraîche

1. Soak the sweetbreads in cold water for 3 hours, changing the water several times during this period.

2. Trim stems from the spinach. Place in 1½ quarts boiling water. Lower heat, cover, and simmer 10 to 15 minutes, or until tender. Remove, rinse under cold water, and drain well. Press dry and set aside.

3. Drain the sweetbreads and place in a saucepan with the wine, leek, celery, onion, and the dill stems; add water to cover. Bring to a boil, lower heat, and simmer for 30 minutes.

4. With a slotted spoon, remove the sweetbreads to a bowl. Boil the wine/leek broth until reduced to one-third. While the broth reduces, pull off and discard the outer membranes of the sweetbreads. Slice into ⅓-inch thick escalopes. Remove and discard any hard, fatty parts. Sauté the escalopes in a large skillet with 4 tablespoons of the butter, the mushrooms, and salt and pepper, until golden brown on both sides.

5. Melt 6 tablespoons of the butter in a saucepan; add the flour and whisk until smooth. Let cook about 3 minutes without browning. Gradually whisk in the hot wine/leek broth. Simmer 5 to 8 minutes over gentle heat, stirring until the sauce is thick and smooth. Stir in the cream and continue to cook, stirring, for about 10 to 15 minutes until the sauce again is thickened. Strain through a cone sieve into a clean saucepan. Finely chop the rest of the dill and add to the saucepan. Keep hot.

(continued next page)

6. Heat the remaining 2 tablespoons butter in a large skillet until nut brown. Add the spinach; season with salt and pepper and toss well over high heat for 1 to 2 minutes. Remove spinach and arrange on a plate in the shape of a crown. Place the sweetbreads in the center and cover with the sauce. Serve at once.

Note: If you decide to use crème fraîche instead of the whipping cream, you can make your own. Mix 2 teaspoons buttermilk with 2 cups raw, heavy cream. Heat to 85° then allow to rest at room temperature until thickened.

We like to hear voices and laughter and see people having a good time!

SALADE LA TORTUE

1 head Bibb lettuce,
   washed and torn
½ head escarole, shredded
1¼ cups julienned celery root

¾ cup diced pimiento
   VINAIGRETTE DRESSING
3 tomatoes, quartered

Combine all ingredients except the tomatoes in a salad bowl. Drizzle the Vinaigrette Dressing over the salad and toss lightly to coat evenly. Arrange the tomato quarters attractively on top. Serve at once.

VINAIGRETTE DRESSING

¾ cup salad oil
¼ cup red wine vinegar
   Pinch of sugar
1 teaspoon Dijon mustard
   Salt and black pepper
   to taste

1 teaspoon minced green
   onion
1 teaspoon minced red
   Spanish onion
1 small clove garlic, crushed

In a jar with a screw-top lid, combine all ingredients. Store in refrigerator to chill and allow flavors to blend. Shake well before using.

In seasoning salads, it is important to use good wine vinegar.

GÂTEAU SAINT-HONORÉ

*PÂTE FEUILLETÉE (see
second page following)*
½ teaspoon salt
1 cup plus 1 teaspoon sugar
½ cup unsalted butter
1 cup flour
5 eggs
1 tablespoon milk
*CRÈME PÂTISSIÈRE (see
third page following)*

1 packet Knox gelatin
4 egg whites
3 tablespoons confectioners'
sugar
Dash of lemon juice
1 cup whipping cream,
well chilled
1 tablespoon superfine sugar
Dash of vanilla extract

1. About 6 hours in advance, prepare the Pâte Feuilletée.

2. While it is chilling, the last 25 minutes, grease two baking sheets.

3. To prepare the pâte à chou, pour 1 cup water in a small saucepan. Add the salt, 1 teaspoon sugar, and the butter; bring to a boil. Add the flour. While beating vigorously, simmer over low heat until the paste leaves the inside of the pan clean. Remove from heat and cool slightly.

4. Break 4 of the eggs one at a time into the cream mixture, beating vigorously after each addition, until the consistency of paste.

5. From this chou paste, make small cream puffs called profiteroles by forming eighteen walnut-shaped balls and placing them at 2-inch intervals on one of the greased baking sheets. Set the remaining chou paste aside.

6. Beat the remaining 1 egg with the milk to create a dorure. Using a pastry brush, brush the profiteroles with some of the dorure.

7. Preheat oven to 425°. Chill a small mixing bowl and electric beaters.

8. Remove the Pâte Feuilletée from the refrigerator. Roll out the dough until ¼-inch thick, and make a tart pastry by cutting a 9 to 10-inch circle. Lay the circle on the second greased baking sheet. Fill a pastry bag with the reserved chou paste and attach a round ½-inch tube. Pipe a border counterclockwise around the edge of the pastry circle. Be sure to move the tip slowly around, pushing

hard on the bag. When the border is completed, move the tip quickly in a continuing counterclockwise swirl toward the center, pressing only lightly on the bag. The border should be higher than the swirl. Brush with the remaining dorure.

9. Place the baking sheets in the preheated oven. Bake 20 to 25 minutes, or until the tart pastry is brown and the profiteroles turn a tannish brown and are firm and crisp.

10. While baking, prepare the Crème Pâtissière. Let about 2½ cups cool to room temperature, stirring from time to time to prevent a crust from forming.

11. Pour the remaining 2 cups of the hot cream into a bowl. Soften the gelatin in 2 tablespoons cold water. Add to the cream and stir until dissolved. Let cool. Beat the egg whites until stiff, gradually adding the confectioners' sugar during the last minute of beating. Fold into the cooled gelatin/cream mixture to create the crème Saint-Honoré. Set aside.

12. When baked, remove the tart pastry and profiteroles from the oven and let cool.

13. Make a small hole in the side of each profiterole with a sharp knife. Using a pastry bag fitted with a small tube, fill the puffs with the reserved, cool crème pâtissière. Set aside.

14. Fill the tart pastry with the crème Saint-Honoré to ¼ inch from the top of the pâte à chou border. Set this gâteau aside.

15. Place the remaining 1 cup sugar with ½ cup water in a saucepan and add the lemon juice. Stirring constantly, bring to a boil and cook until the consistency of caramel syrup. Immediately dip the tops of the profiteroles in the hot syrup; let cool to solidify. When cooled, dip the bottoms in the syrup and stick close together on the pâte à chou border of the gâteau.

16. With the chilled bowl and beaters, whip the cream until stiff, gradually incorporating the superfine sugar and vanilla extract. Fill a pastry bag with the whipped cream and pipe an attractive pattern over the gâteau. Chill ½ hour before serving.

LA TORTUE

PÂTE FEUILLETÉE

4 *cups flour*
1 *teaspoon salt*
1½ *cups ice water*
  (approximately)

1 *pound unsalted butter,*
  chilled

1. Sift the flour and the salt over a pastry board. Make a well in the center and pour in 1 cup ice water. Mix gently and quickly, taking care not to knead the dough. Add up to ½ cup ice water a little at a time to create a paste with a firm texture. (It is most important to add only a very small amount of water as necessary and to work the dough as little as possible.) Lightly shape the dough into a ball, place in a bowl and chill 15 to 20 minutes.
2. Meanwhile, place the butter in a bowl of ice water and knead until it softens. Remove and squeeze out water. Be sure at this point the butter and chilled dough are the same consistency.
3. Place the dough on a lightly floured surface. Roll into a rough square about ¼ inch thick. Place the butter in the center of the square of dough. Fold the dough around the butter, so that the butter is completely encased. Wrap dough in plastic wrap or waxed paper and chill 25 minutes.
4. Lightly roll the dough into a long rectangle about ½ inch thick; do not let the butter come through the dough. Position the dough so that the long side faces you. Fold one-third of the dough over the center third. Fold the remaining third over the other two to form three layers. Turn the dough so that the top flap faces you. (This procedure completes one turn.) Roll into another long rectangle. Fold into thirds a second time and chill 25 minutes.
5. Repeat step 4 to complete four turns in all. Wrap and chill 25 minutes.

Note: If you wish to make the Pâte Feuilletée days in advance, complete the first two turns, wrap well, and refrigerate. When ready to use, make the last two turns, then roll out to a ¼-inch thickness for cutting the pastry circle.

LA TORTUE

CRÈME PÂTISSIÈRE

6 egg yolks
1 cup plus 2 tablespoons
sugar
½ cup plus 1 teaspoon flour

3 cups milk
1 (1½") piece vanilla bean
Pinch of salt

1. Beat the yolks with the sugar in a small mixing bowl until very pale and light. Add the flour and beat just until smooth. Carefully pour into a saucepan.
2. Place the milk and piece of vanilla bean in another saucepan and scald. Remove the bean. Slowly pour the scalded milk into the egg mixture, stirring constantly. Add the salt and place over low heat. Cook, stirring vigorously with a wire whisk, until the cream almost comes to a boil. Cook 2 to 3 minutes further, making sure the cream does not boil. Remove from heat and strain through a chinois.

Willows

Dinner for Six

Cold Cherry Soup

Poached Turbot on Sautéed Spinach

Veal Tournedos and Sweetbreads in Armagnac Sauce

Saffron Rice

Green Beans and Carrots

Chocolate Soufflé with Pear Sauce

Wines:

With the Turbot—Joseph Phelps Johannisberg Riesling, Early Harvest
With the Tournedos—Simi Sonoma Zinfandel

Abdul Suliman, General Manager
David Beechman, Food and Beverages Manager
David Bidwell, Executive Chef

WILLOWS

Enter the Willows and leave mid-America behind. Enter a world where stylish transcends the trendy—a world of club-like cosmopolitan chic. Pewter velvet dresses its walls and cushions the curved banquettes. Under smokey glass ceilings, dark mirrored columns create alcoves which are intimate yet separated from the pulse of the room. Table appointments glow in warm peach tones; fresh flowers, poppy-patterned service plates, and delicate crystal complete the look and feel of elegance.

A cocoon of luxe within the Nicollet Mall Hyatt Regency, the Willows is not locked into a corporate conception. Beyond the international Hyatt's insistence on fresh foods and prime viands, it has a character all its own. And the philosophy that informs it is deceptively simple: the finest of cuisine prepared and served by people who care.

Waiters in gray coats guide the diner in selecting from succulent entrées, such as the Willow's forte: spit-roasted duck with sauceboats of savory or sweet fruity toppings. Or, the diner is tempted by such other uncommon entrées as pheasant en croûte stuffed with lingonberries; quail and veal tenderloin sauced with green peppercorns, fresh scallops, and Dover sole; and lamb loin in sabayon sauce.

The waiters, who nightly taste new dishes, maintain a fresh interest in the foods they serve. And the service is exemplary, as they keep the citrus-scented goblets brimming with bottled water and recommend a wine with skilled familiarity. Coffee service, indeed, is not a neglected performance at the Willows. After a dessert buffet of puff pastry and buttercream, the delighted diner is served a special Kona brew along with pots of freshly whipped cream and salvers of chocolate bits, zest of orange, and sugar. As final gracenote, ladies receive a long-stemmed flower from the evening's gray-liveried *Rosenkavalier*—a finishing touch that makes an evening out at the Willows one that is memorable.

Hyatt Regency Hotel
1300 Nicollet Mall
Minneapolis

WILLOWS

COLD CHERRY SOUP

6 *pints bing cherries, pitted*	1 *cup plain yogurt or*
1 *cup orange juice*	*sour cream*
2 *cloves*	12 *leaves fresh mint*
1 *stick cinnamon*	¼ *cup whipping cream,*
2 *tablespoons sugar*	*lightly whipped*
1 to 2 *tablespoons Grand Marnier*	

1. In a saucepan over medium heat, place the cherries, orange juice, cloves, cinnamon, and sugar. Bring to a boil; then simmer for 1 to 2 minutes to develop the flavor. Remove the cloves and cinnamon stick.

2. Allow to cool slightly, then purée in a blender. Add up to 2 tablespoons Grand Marnier to taste. Stir in the yogurt or sour cream. Cover and chill overnight in the refrigerator.

3. To serve, ladle the soup into individual serving bowls. Garnish with the mint leaves; float a spoonful of the whipped cream on top.

We want to stay ahead of our customers—to provide quality both in atmosphere and in food.

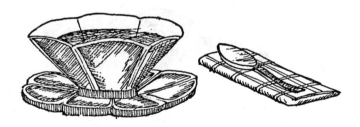

WILLOWS

POACHED TURBOT ON SAUTÉED SPINACH

COURT BOUILLON
6 (6-ounce) turbot fillets
2 tablespoons butter
½ pound fresh spinach,
    washed

2 tablespoons chopped
    shallots
RASBPERRY BEURRE
    BLANC
½ cup fresh raspberries

1. In a heavy skillet, heat the Court Bouillon over medium heat until simmering. Poach the turbot in this liquid just until flaky, approximately 5 minutes.

2. Meanwhile, in a sauté pan, heat the butter over medium heat and sauté the spinach and shallots 3 minutes or until wilted.

3. To serve, arrange the spinach to cover a serving platter. Remove the turbot from the poaching liquid and place it in the center of the spinach, so that the green leaves are visible around the edge of the plate. Ladle the Raspberry Beurre Blanc over the top. Garnish with the fresh raspberries arranged attractively over the turbot. Serve immediately.

COURT BOUILLON

1 cup white wine
7 cups water
1½ teaspoons whole black
    peppercorns
1 small bay leaf
1 teaspoon sea salt or
    regular salt

½ stalk celery, coarsely
    chopped
½ carrot, coarsely chopped
½ onion, coarsely chopped
1 sprig fresh thyme, or ½
    teaspoon dried thyme

Combine all ingredients in a large saucepan. Bring to a boil. Lower heat and cook until reduced to 2 to 3 cups.

RASPBERRY BEURRE BLANC

¼ cup raspberry vinegar
¼ cup white wine
1 tablespoon chopped shallots
1 bay leaf

¼ cup whipping cream
½ cup unsalted butter
    Salt and pepper

1. In a saucepan, combine the vinegar, wine, shallots, and bay leaf. Cook over medium heat until the liquid is almost evaporated, approximately 3 minutes. Add the cream and continue to cook until the cream is reduced to a little over half, approximately 2 minutes. Remove from heat.
2. Slowly blend in the butter, adding small pieces one at a time. Strain the sauce through a sieve lined with dampened cheesecloth; add salt and pepper to taste.

With freshness we make no compromise. Our purveyors are very aware of it.

VEAL TOURNEDOS AND SWEETBREADS IN ARMAGNAC SAUCE

¾ cup butter
6 (4-ounce) medallions of veal cut from loin or rack
1 pound veal sweetbreads (approximately)
½ cup flour
1 egg, beaten
2 tablespoons chopped shallots
2 tablespoons white wine
1½ cups whipping cream

1 tablespoon freshly chopped chives
1 tablespoon Armagnac
Salt and pepper
6 (1-inch) slices whole wheat bread
2 tablespoons Pommery mustard
2 tablespoons glace de viande

1. In a large skillet, heat ¼ cup of the butter. Sauté the veal medallions over medium heat until medium rare, approximately 3 minutes on each side, turning once. Remove from the pan and keep warm; reserve the pan to make the Armagnac sauce.

2. Meanwhile, place the sweetbreads in a stockpot and add water to cover. Boil over medium heat 15 to 20 minutes, or until they turn white. Drain; clean out veins and membranes and discard. Dust sweetbreads in the flour, then dip in the beaten egg.

3. Heat ¼ cup of the butter in a sauté pan and sauté the sweetbreads over medium heat until they turn a golden brown, approximately 2 minutes on each side.

4. In the pan used to sauté the veal, place the shallots and sauté slightly over medium heat, approximately 1 minute. Add the wine and deglaze for 1 minute. Add the cream and the chives and continue to cook until mixture is reduced by half, approximately 5 minutes. Sprinkle the Armagnac on the sauce and stir to mix. Season with salt and pepper to taste.

5. Heat the remaining ¼ cup butter in the sauté pan over medium heat and make croutons by sautéeing the bread approximately 1 minute on each side.

6. To serve, place a crouton on each plate and spread with the mustard. Place a veal medallion on the crouton and arrange sweetbreads on either side. Ladle some of the Armagnac sauce over the sweetbreads and spoon a little glace de viande on the veal. Serve at once.

Glace de viande, or meat glaze, may be purchased at gourmet stores.

I've become enchanted with fresh herbs. Once you use those, you can't go back and get your flavor out of a bottle.

SAFFRON RICE

2 tablespoons butter	2 cups Chicken Stock
¼ cup chopped onion	(see index)
1 cup white rice	Pinch of saffron
2 tablespoons white wine	

1. Preheat oven to 350°.
2. In a saucepan, heat the butter over medium heat and sauté the onion until limp, approximately 3 minutes. Add the rice; stir to mix and add the wine to deglaze the mixture. Add the chicken stock and the pinch of saffron and bring to a boil. Stir and remove from heat.
3. Cover the saucepan and bake the rice in a preheated oven until all the moisture is absorbed, approximately 15 to 20 minutes. Serve hot in small individual bowls.

The Hyatt believes in creativity and daring. Yet of all their restaurants, there is only one Willows. And that's here in Minneapolis!

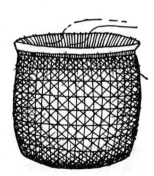

GREEN BEANS AND CARROTS

1 pound French green beans	2 tablespoons hazelnut oil
3 large carrots	Salt and pepper

1. Clean the beans and snap off the ends. Steam the beans in a small saucepan with ¼ cup water until just tender, approximately 5 minutes. Immediately plunge them into ice water to retain their bright green color; drain at once and keep warm.
2. Meanwhile, cut the carrots into fine julienne strips the length of the green beans. In a small sauté pan, heat the oil over medium heat and sauté the carrots until al dente, approximately 3 minutes. Add the green beans and reheat briefly. Season to taste with salt and pepper.
3. Divide the vegetables among six individual serving plates, and serve at once.

In preparing the vegetables, the bottom line is al dente.

CHOCOLATE SOUFFLÉ WITH PEAR SAUCE

¼ pound butter (approximately)	3 (1-ounce) squares grated unsweetened chocolate
½ cup sugar (approximately)	8 egg whites
7 tablespoons flour	Pinch of salt
2 cups milk	PEAR SAUCE
4 egg yolks	

1. Preheat oven to 375°.
2. Butter six individual soufflé dishes and the rims with 2 tablespoons of the butter. Sprinkle with 2 tablespoons of the sugar to coat thoroughly.
3. In a saucepan, melt the remaining 6 tablespoons butter over low heat; add the flour, whisking together, and cook for 1 to 2 minutes, until the flour flavor disappears. Remove from heat
4. Add the milk and the remaining 6 tablespoons sugar, whisking constantly. Return to medium heat and cook, whisking, until the mixture thickens, approximately 3 minutes.

5. Remove from heat and add the egg yolks one at a time, whisking briskly. Add the grated chocolate and continue whisking until the chocolate melts and blends. Set aside.

6. In the large, clean bowl of an electric mixer, beat the egg whites with the salt until stiff but not dry. Stir a small spoonful into the chocolate batter to facilitate blending; then gently fold in the remaining egg whites.

7. Gently pour the soufflé into the prepared dishes. Place the dishes into a pan of hot water to 1 inch in depth and bake in preheated oven 30 to 40 minutes, until the tops brown. Serve immediately with the Pear Sauce.

PEAR SAUCE

6 tablespoons butter
7 tablespoons flour
3 cups milk
6 tablespoons sugar
2 tablespoons Poire William liqueur

1 to 3 tablespoons whipping cream (optional)
1 square dark chocolate (sweetened or unsweetened), shaved

1. In a saucepan over medium heat, melt the butter and add the flour, whisking together; cook for 1 to 2 minutes, until the flour flavor disappears. Remove from heat.

2. Add the milk and sugar, whisking until blended. Return to medium heat and cook until thickened, approximately 3 minutes.

3. Remove from heat and add the liqueur. Dilute with the cream, if desired. Turn into a serving tureen and sprinkle with grated chocolate. Serve with the chocolate soufflé.

We do serve our soufflés from a cart. Other than that, there's no tableside work. Food comes first here, not theatrics. Those tasks belong in the kitchen.

Appetizers

Breads and Doughs

Desserts and Dessert Accents

Entrées

RECIPE INDEX

THE GREAT CHEFS SERIES

A Collection of Gourmet Recipes from the Finest Chefs in the Country

Each book contains gourmet recipes for complete meals from the chefs of 21 great restaurants.

____ *Dining In–Baltimore*	$7.95	____ *Dining In–Monterey Peninsula*	$7.95
____ *Dining In–Boston*	8.95	____ *Dining In–Philadelphia*	8.95
____ *Dining In–Chicago, Vol. II*	8.95	____ *Dining In–Phoenix*	8.95
____ *Dining In–Cleveland*	8.95	____ *Dining In–Pittsburgh*	7.95
____ *Dining In–Dallas, Revised*	8.95	____ *Dining In–Portland*	7.95
____ *Dining In–Denver*	7.95	____ *Dining In–St. Louis*	7.95
____ *Dining In–Hawaii*	7.95	____ *Dining In–San Francisco*	7.95
____ *Dining In–Houston, Vol. I*	7.95	____ *Dining In–Seattle, Vol. III*	8.95
____ *Dining In–Houston, Vol. II*	7.95	____ *Dining In–Sun Valley*	7.95
____ *Dining In–Kansas City*	7.95	____ *Dining In–Toronto*	7.95
____ *Dining In–Los Angeles*	7.95	____ *Dining In–Vancouver, B.C.*	8.95
____ *Dining In–Manhattan*	8.95	____ *Dining In–Washington, D.C.*	8.95
____ *Dining In–Milwaukee*	7.95	____ *Feasting In Atlanta*	7.95
____ *Dining In–Minneapolis/St. Paul, Vol. II* 8.95		____ *Feasting In New Orleans*	7.95

☐ CHECK HERE IF YOU WOULD LIKE TO HAVE A
DIFFERENT DINING IN–COOKBOOK SENT TO YOU
ONCE A MONTH

Payable by MasterCard, Visa, or C.O.D. Returnable if not satisfied.
List price plus $1.00 postage and handling for each book.

BILL TO: **SHIP TO:**

Name _____   Name _____

Address _____   Address _____

City _____ State ____ Zip _____   City _____ State ____ Zip _____

☐ Payment enclosed   ☐ Send C.O.D.   ☐ Charge

Visa # _____ Exp. Date _____

MasterCard # _____ Exp. Date _____

Signature _____ _____

PEANUT BUTTER PUBLISHING

2445 76th Avenue S.E. • Mercer Island, WA 98040
(206) 236-1982